What People Are Saying About Mike Broomhead

"You won't forget Mike Broomhead's story of rising up from poverty and becoming one of the leading voices in talk radio. He offers common sense advice and a unique take on life, relationships, and politics. I am proud to call him a friend."

—GLENN BECK, radio and TV host

"Mike Broomhead gets it. Quality of life pivots upon an optimum situational awareness and thrives when embracing truth, logic, and common sense, and the evidence to support them. Having shared the radio microphone with Mike on many occasions, hammering home this political correctness-smashing truth crowbar, and hanging backstage at the world's greatest rock-and-roll events (mine), there is no doubt that Mike is a true American warrior in the culture war, rock solid in the asset column with the greatest Americans out here."

—TED NUGENT, rock-and-roll legend

"An inspiring book by a man who continues to encourage people every day to know what they believe and how to stand up for what is right. My friend Mike Broomhead has learned a thing or two about life—and we get the benefit of learning these life lessons too through these pages!"

—MAC POWELL, lead singer of Third Day

IF YOU'RE GONNA BE DUMB, YOU BETTER BE TOUGH

LESSONS FROM MY LIFE WITH BULLS, PROTESTERS, AND POLITICIANS

MIKE BROOMHEAD

WITH LISA DE PASQUALE

A POST HILL PRESS BOOK

If You're Gonna Be Dumb, You Better Be Tough:
Lessons from My Life with Bulls, Protesters, and Politicians
© 2018 by Mike Broomhead
All Rights Reserved

ISBN: 978-1-68261-805-9
ISBN (eBook): 978-1-68261-806-6

Cover art by Cody Corcoran
Interior design and composition by Greg Johnson, Textbook Perfect

Post Hill Press
New York • Nashville
posthillpress.com

Published in the United States of America

TABLE OF CONTENTS

INVEST IN MEANINGFUL RELATIONSHIPS

I WAS BORN IN NEWBURY, Ohio, a farm town not too far from Cleveland. I made a trip back to Cleveland for the Republican National Convention when Donald Trump was nominated. The hotel where we stayed was about twenty miles from the town where I lived until age nine. I went to my old neighborhood and I found my old house. I found my grandparents' house. My grandparents' house wasn't particularly familiar, because I hadn't been there since we moved over forty years ago. Then I turned a corner and saw a lake. I thought, "Wait, I know this place. This is where my grandfather taught me to fish."

When I was at the lake, I closed my eyes, feeling the summer breeze, and it felt like I was riding my bike there. It all came flooding back.

My father was an alcoholic. There's really no nice way to say it. I had a very strained relationship with him even though I wasn't fully aware of his condition as a young kid. When he

1

was around, he just wasn't someone I wanted to be around. We didn't do the typical father-son activities. In hindsight, I know my grandfather, my mother's father, knew that and made up for it in ways that still benefit me today.

My grandparents' house and my parents' house backed up to each other. We both had two acres in our backyard that were overgrown with weeds. We lived on Thomas Street, and they lived one street over on Grace Street. My brother's name was Thomas, so it was like he had a street named after him. One day, my grandfather took his tractor through the overgrown weeds and cut a trail from his street to ours. He then went out and built a street sign that read, "Michael Road." Now I had a street named after me, too. At five years old, I thought that was a big deal.

My grandfather's name was Francis and, of course, everyone called him Frank. I was his best buddy. That's the kind of relationship we had. I would get up in the morning and walk down Michael Road to my grandfather's house. We would eat breakfast together. We'd eat lunch together. We'd sit in his living room and watch game shows and *Hee Haw* on TV. He sat in his rocking chair, and I sat in his lap when I was still little. We didn't have much, but when I think of family heirlooms, that old rocking chair is the only one that matters.

One of our favorite activities was fishing. We would take old folding chairs and sit in the backyard. Then we would throw metal garbage can lids like Frisbees into the yard. We would practice with fishing poles, casting into the lids and reeling them back. Of course, he had better things to do, but he made me feel like I was the only person he wanted to be with in the world.

My grandfather was a retired Chevy mechanic. He was a homebody, but he still did some work fixing neighbors' cars after

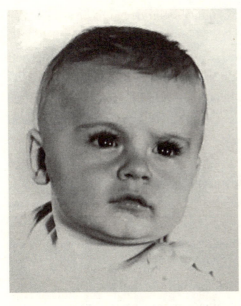

Even as a baby, I looked like trouble.

he retired. There is no doubt I get my work ethic from him. As a young boy, it was a thrill to just hand him tools while he fiddled around on a car in his jeans and white undershirt. He'd build trailers for farmers' tractors. He would fix the neighbors' stuff. He did it because it kept him busy, not necessarily because he needed the money. He could build anything. We would go to the junkyard to buy parts. He would drive me around in an old Chevy. This was in the "good ol' days," so I would stand on the seat next to him when he drove. Can you imagine if you saw a kid doing that now? The car is long gone, but I still have the keys to that old Chevy.

Now my grandmother was the sweetest little Polish woman in the world. She just loved all over us all of the time and spoiled us rotten. At that age, my brother Tom and I were hellions. My mother would try to discipline us, but our grandmother would say, "Ah, let them, let them."

My grandmother was a housewife and a homemaker, and she did everything a housewife in the 1960s and 1970s did. My grandfather earned the living; my grandmother kept the house. They didn't live in a big, fancy house, but it was always clean. Every day, she would cook lunch for my grandfather and me. As we sat and watched game shows, my grandmother would be in the kitchen cooking amazing Polish food. She would bring lunch to us on TV trays. There was always something to eat, and it was always cooked from scratch. There was always a piece of cake or pie. She enjoyed being a housewife and providing in the way that she could.

My grandparents grew up during the Depression, so we would eat the strangest things, as they wanted to squeeze the most out of everything they had because there was a time when they had nothing. Consequently, my grandfather would always make me try stuff that was both "offal" and *awful.* On more than one occasion, it was hard to eat it after I found out what it was, but it always was delicious because my grandmother cooked it.

When I was nine, my grandfather was sent home from the hospital because he was dying. A hospital bed was set up in his living room next to his rocking chair. Weeks before my grandfather died, he was on so many drugs just to keep him comfortable. On my youngest brother's second birthday, my mother put him on the bed and my grandfather sang "Happy Birthday" to my brother. Everybody cried, because they knew that this was the last birthday in the family that my grandfather would see.

He was the patriarch of the family, and then he was gone.

The time he invested in me made me want to be the kind of man he was to my own family. When you feel other people are invested in you, it gives you self-worth and purpose. It also compels you to want to do the same and invest in other people. I thank God for those years with my grandfather. As good as it was with him in Ohio is as bad as it was with my father when we moved to Florida.

HOW TO CHANGE A TIRE

THERE'S A REAL SENSE of independence in fixing the things around your house that need to be fixed. When the garbage disposal goes out, are you going to call the plumber or are you going to figure out how to take the garbage disposal out and replace it? Many people have the luxury of being able to call a plumber when they need to, but there's satisfaction in at least being able to diagnose a problem. You can figure it out if you have a basic knowledge of tools and how things work. I would love for my grandkids to have their own toolboxes so they know they've got the tools to do the job themselves.

Not too long ago, I watched a documentary on one of the medical channels. Orthopedic surgeons were replacing a guy's knee. They cut him open. They used a saw to cut his knee at the fibula and at the femur. They used a drill and drilled a hole in the middle of the fibula. They drilled another hole in the femur. They took a hammer and pounded screws into both. Then, they took the new knee and used the same hammer to hammer it in place. Finally, they attached the ligaments and sealed the guy shut.

When it was over, I thought, "Those are the same tools I use to build somebody's house." They were a hammer and a drill. They were the same basic tools. Granted, they're a lot more technologically advanced, but it's physical labor along with the knowledge of how to use the tools you have—whether you're building a staircase or you're building some guy's brand-new knee.

Life is funny, because if there is one thing that would disappoint my grandfather, it's that I am a die-hard Ford guy. As a onetime Chevy mechanic, he would spin in his grave.

I learned how to use tools by watching him work on cars and handing him his tools. I still don't know a whole lot about working on cars, but I know tools. I remember him telling me in the early 1970s, "Mike, you better learn how to work on cars, because by the time you're old enough to buy a new car, they are going to cost five thousand dollars!"

I think of that and have to laugh, because five thousand dollars didn't even pay the taxes on the last vehicle I bought. In that day and age, that was the thinking: If you're going to own something expensive, you'd better know how it works and how to fix it.

Previous generations, such as my grandfather's, diagnosed everything by process of elimination. First, you would try to start the car. If it didn't start, you would start at the carburetor. If it wasn't the carburetor, you would move to the next thing. Was it the starter that was bad? You had to know what you were looking at and what it sounded like. Even sometimes what it smelled like! That's how he could tell, and that's how he fixed things. He was just a genius at it, like many men of his generation.

Now we can take our cars to mechanics; they hook them up to a computer and it tells them what's wrong. There are still some basics that everyone should know, and one of them is how to change a tire. I would never let my kids or grandkids leave the house in a vehicle alone unless they knew that basic skill. It's a safety issue more than anything. If they're stuck, they need to know what to do if they don't have cell phone power or service. Of course, when they do have cell service, they call me, so I will change their tire for them. They are smart enough to know how to do something for themselves, but also whom to call when they're in trouble.

I spent only a few weeks in the Boy Scouts (more on that later), but the one thing I remember is to be prepared. So, be sure you have all the tools in your vehicle to be able to fix a tire. This includes a spare tire that's checked regularly for proper inflation, a lug wrench, a jack, gloves, wheel wedges, safety flares, a tire pressure gauge, and a flashlight with good batteries or one that's solar-powered.

First, pull over to a safe spot. Ideally, it would be a side street or shoulder of an off-ramp if you are on a highway. Look for a place within safe driving distance that will get you out of traffic. Obviously, you don't want to be in an area where you might be in someone's blind spot, such as around a corner or on a side of the road that would put you on the traffic side. The best conditions are a flat road with no incline and on well-lit pavement.

Next, remove your spare and the tools you'll need. If it's dark, put out flares or reflective triangles so people can see you. Put wedges on the tire opposite the tire you're changing, for stability. If the tire's lug nuts aren't exposed, remove the tire cover or hubcap. Use the lug wrench to loosen (not remove) the nuts. Put the jack in a place that's directly under the vehicle's frame. Usually the lug wrench can be used as the crank for the jack. Crank the jack until the tire is about six inches above the pavement.

Once the tire is off the ground, remove the lug nuts and put them someplace safe so you don't have to fumble around looking for them later. Remove the flat tire and put it out of the way. Place the new tire on by lining up the spare with the lug bolts. Screw on the lug nuts by hand. Don't tighten with the lug wrench until after the spare is lowered to the ground. Crank the jack down until the tire is on the ground. Then tighten the lug nuts with the lug wrench. Start by tightening every other one and really put some muscle into it. After you've worked up a sweat, replace the tire cover or hubcap if you have one. Remove the wedges from the opposite tire and load all your tools and flat tire back into your vehicle. If it's been a while since you've checked your spare's air pressure, go ahead and do that. The proper tire pressure for your car can usually be found on a sticker on the bottom of the driver's or passenger's door. It's also helpful to keep a can of aerosol tire inflator in case there is an issue. Once you're back on the road, get both tires checked and replace any if needed.

My grandfather was a man's man and took great care of the people he loved. One day when I was nine years old and he knew he was dying of bladder cancer, he pulled me aside. Knowing my father was effectively not part of our family and that I was the oldest of my brothers, he talked to me about being a man and taking care of my family. It gives me great pleasure to be there for my family now and to pass on some of the skills he taught me to my kids and now to you.

I want my kids and grandkids to feel the same sense of independence and satisfaction my grandfather felt from fixing things. Not only are these good skills to have, but they're also a common thread that connects our family's generations.

IT'S OKAY TO LAUGH AT A FUNERAL

MY GRANDFATHER FRANK was the guy everybody rallied around. At a family funeral for one of my mother's uncles, there was a little kitchenette in the basement where people would sit and have coffee during the viewing. The viewing was upstairs. A good group of people was in the basement, where my grandfather was holding court, and the laughter rose up to the viewing area. He was telling stories and jokes. One family member came down and said, "Hey, Frank, you have to stop. The people upstairs are mad because everybody is down here having a good time."

In less than ten minutes, he could turn a funeral into a party. He didn't mean any disrespect by it. It was just the way he was. He was very irreverent, but at the same time, very respectful. I appreciate that dichotomy more as I get older. Things didn't offend Frank, because he didn't take life too seriously.

I'm proud to say I got my sense of humor from him. I have never heard a joke that I don't remember. Just like my grandfather, I can recite on command every clean and dirty joke I have ever heard in my life. Like many fathers and grandfathers, he told the same jokes over and over again. But he always had a new one every time I saw him. The jokes were just dumb enough to be funny when you're six years old. For example:

"Why do Eskimos wash their clothes in Tide?"

"Because it's too cold out-tide."

Did I go to school the next day and tell that joke? Of course. I actually told that joke just the other day. If my grandfather is looking down at me telling his jokes to people, that would make him feel good.

At the funeral where my grandfather got in trouble, he turned to my mom and said, "Rose, when I die, I want you to bury me with my ass hanging out of the ground, so Mike's got a place to park his bike when he visits."

My grandfather was very self-deprecating and, as I mentioned, very irreverent. He genuinely would have wanted people to laugh at his funeral. He wouldn't have wanted you to feel somber and sad. He wanted you to remember him in the ways he made you laugh. And we did.

I was raised Catholic and I was an altar boy, so I was an altar boy at my grandfather's funeral. It was one of the biggest honors of my life. At my grandfather's funeral, all the adults sat around and said, "Remember when Frank would…?" We all laughed, and it was a tribute to him. My grandfather was gone, but he was still holding court in his own way.

EMBRACE RESPONSIBILITY, BUT NOT TOO QUICKLY

GROWING UP, I WAS A LONER. I was antisocial because I worked from an early age and just grew up fast. I was very independent and very hardheaded.

I got my first non-paperboy type job at a dirty Chinese restaurant when I was twelve. They didn't care about my age because they paid me under the table. I used the money to buy my own clothes so that I could buy what I wanted. It wasn't a ton of money since I was just a busboy, but it was enough to go out with my friends without having to ask my parents for money. Then when I was fifteen, there was a brand-new restaurant opening in town. You had to be sixteen to work there. I lied on my job application to get that job. Most kids lie about their age so they can drink or smoke; I lied so I could work. I did every job in the place except for bartending because I was too young.

On school nights, I would work until midnight or two o'clock in the morning. Then after working late, I wouldn't go to school. Of course, I got horrible grades.

Then my mom kicked me out at fifteen and I was on my own. I got a roommate and an apartment. I don't blame her. I was a little shit and worst of all, I was not setting a good example for my younger brothers.

By the time I turned seventeen, my behavior at school hadn't improved and I was basically encouraged to leave after skipping school for twenty days in a row. They didn't kick me out, but the dean of students said, "You know, high school's not for everyone."

So I left. I joined the Army in November of 1984 and planned to get my GED when I enlisted. Unfortunately, I blew out my knee and was out of the Army by February of 1985. So I went to back to work. I eventually took my GED test and the certificate came in the mail within a day or two of my class's graduation. I guess you could say I got to where I needed to be even though it was a rocky path. A week later, I went to work as an electrical apprentice.

After I got out of the Army, I moved back home with my mom. I straightened out a little bit, plus she felt guilty as hell for kicking me out. We became closer. When I was a little boy, I was her little helper because I was the oldest boy. That changed as I got older and became just an angry guy, and she didn't know how to handle me. She was struggling herself working seventy hours a week just to make a living. I was running around and she couldn't control me. It just was horrible for both of us. Thankfully, our relationship got better. My mom's my hero now, and

I feel guilty about a lot of what I did. Now there are no regrets about things that were left unsaid.

There was never a time when I didn't feel like a grown-up. I was always making my way, making a living, and figuring out how to take care of myself. That, along with wanting to be a good example for my younger brothers, is what saved me from going off the deep end. I never felt like I was impacted by peer pressure. I had enough self-reliance or self-restraint to not feel compelled to do something I didn't want to do. I also had really good friends who respected my choices. If they didn't like me because of my choice not to do something, I wouldn't have wanted to be their friend anyway.

That confidence to be my own man came from my grandfather. He was the type of guy who didn't allow me to make excuses. If I were to say, "Well, my friend did it," he would say, "I don't care what they do. I care what you do."

I've never been arrested. I never had any reason to be arrested. I've had friends who were criminals, but I've never done anything like that. Like a lot of kids in high school, my friends and I would drink and go to parties. I wasn't a juvenile delinquent, and given my childhood, I had the cards stacked against me on that front.

There was definitely a price that came with growing up so fast. I was a good athlete. I did it all—wrestling, football, and baseball. I played football on one of the biggest powerhouse Pop Warner football teams in the country when I was twelve to fourteen years old. We were called the Fort Myers Rebels. Our mascot was a Confederate soldier. Black and white kids wore the uniform proudly because we were among the best. On our helmets was an "R." We all had to dress in blue blazers and khaki pants when we traveled to games. We had to wear a blazer with a rebel patch sewn on it. They were already preparing us for college and the pros down to the last detail.

Two-time Super Bowl champion Deion Sanders and I were teammates playing Pop Warner football. Deion was first noticed by Florida State booster and Fort Myers resident Walter Grace, when Deion was playing on our team. Back then, the National Collegiate Athletic Association (NCAA) allowed alumni to recruit.

Of course, it's not just the sports that were important. I am much more appreciative of education. I would love to have the discipline to do the coursework to get an American history degree. To be honest (and maybe this is being somewhat arrogant), I would put my knowledge of American history up against a lot of people's any day of the week, just because of my self-education. However, there is a real accomplishment in earning a diploma, and dedicating yourself to a goal and achieving it.

A part of me would go back to being twelve, and rather than work in a restaurant, I would stick with sports and my education. I would love to know if I could have excelled as an athlete and what types of friendships I could have built. Could I have gotten a college scholarship?

I gave all that up because I just wanted to grow up and be independent. If there was one piece of advice I wish somebody would've instilled in me, it would be to enjoy who I am and where I am. I didn't get that advice then, but I'm grateful I can give it now with honesty and conviction.

DON'T DO THE WRONG THING FOR THE RIGHT REASONS

I HAD A BEER CAN COLLECTION like kids did back in the 1970s. You could get them from all over the world. My dad was a drunk, so it was pretty easy to get him to buy beer. He would buy odd brands of beer, guzzle them, and I'd take the cans.

He was a dispatcher for a big trucking company. He wouldn't drink during the day, but he would come home and get drunk. Then on the weekends, he'd be completely wasted.

Despite my killer beer can collection, there was no benefit to having a drunk for a dad. One day when I was working at the restaurant, he showed up drunk as hell and acting like a tough guy. It was embarrassing. It bothered me because he would show up at my job and make a fool of himself. One of the reasons I got a job when I was twelve is because I wanted to get out of my house. I thought if I could have a job, then I could have my own life. Then he would show up, and that escape from my home life would be gone.

As the oldest, I'm the one who fought through the mountain of garbage with him. He usually wasn't physically abusive. He was physical, but he didn't get abusive to the point where he left marks. One night when he was really drunk, my youngest brother, Bryan, did something wrong. He spanked Bryan with a belt and it definitely got out of hand. I said, "Hit him one more time and you're dead." I knew that I wasn't going to kill him, but I would rather have him coming at me than whale on Bryan. He snapped out of it and gave me a dirty look. I continued to stare at him and challenged him again, "Do it." I was scared, but it didn't matter. He backed off that night.

I looked out for my mom and brothers because I saw what a derelict my dad was. I had no use for him. I was lucky that early in life, my grandfather showed me what a real man should be. So, when I saw my dad's behavior, I thought, what kind of gutless man behaves this way to his family?

My mom stuck around because she thought she should for the kids. Finally, one day I lost it and told her that she needed to get the hell out of there. I told her she needed to get out of where she was because we were in a bad place. I think she realized then that she was doing the wrong thing for the right reasons. It was almost like I was giving her permission to leave. So, she got out of there. It was a huge testament to her strength, because it wasn't easy or necessarily accepted to be a single mother with three boys back then.

My dad was very selfish about the whole thing, which wasn't a surprise. My mom never got any alimony or child support. He stayed in a three-bedroom house with two empty bedrooms all by himself, and we moved to a rathole apartment. He eventually lost his job and almost lost the house. My mom had to beg to get

From left: Tom, Bryan, and me.

out of the lease. We moved back into the house until the house was sold, then moved out again.

My mom never took help from the government. She was never on food stamps and never got any government assistance of any kind. She worked instead. We did get help from people we knew. Once one of my mom's friends came over with a trunkful of groceries. We helped my mom's friend bring them inside, and she left before my mom got home from work. Friends filled our refrigerator and cupboards with groceries. We would also go to the day-old bread store. (It's probably not a coincidence that now I throw out food the second it hits the expiration date.)

My mom was a housewife until the divorce. She didn't have any marketable job skills but had to immediately start working out of necessity. She found work as a receptionist at a real estate office, and then she would clean the office at night for extra money. She would also clean condos and houses that were sold or rented by the real estate office before people moved into them. She was industrious and willing to do anything to keep the three of us boys fed, clothed, and with a roof over our heads.

I was around fourteen at that time and working, so I bought all my own clothes, stuff for school, and anything else I wanted that I could afford. That way, she could focus just on my brothers.

We were all particular about what we wanted to wear. Name-brand clothes mattered in school and we almost never were able to get them. But eventually, I would go and buy what I wanted. I was the eighties king. I was wearing Ocean Pacific T-shirts, Levi's 501s, Reebok sneakers, Gargoyles 44 Blues, a Members Only jacket, and, of course, I had a mullet.

But my mom would get her clothes from coworkers. It didn't really dawn on me until much later that it must have been embarrassing for her on some level to wear coworkers' hand-me-downs at work. I'm sure her coworkers were very happy that she could use them and felt like they were really helping her, which they were. She wore their old clothes so she didn't have to go out and buy clothes for herself, and instead could provide for her kids.

My mom's sacrifice and courage still inspire me every day. Ironically, now that I can afford whatever I want, I wear jeans and seven-dollar T-shirts from H&M every day.

DO AS I SAY, NOT AS I DID

MY CRAZY FRIEND LIVED around the corner from me. Our group of friends affectionately call him crazy. When he joined the Boy Scouts, so did I. I figured I liked being outside and doing stuff, so it would be a good fit. It was fun, but I didn't know anything about the Boy Scouts and the faith-based structure behind the organization. He and I were a couple of maniacs who just wanted to go out into the woods and camp. It wasn't long before we got into trouble.

A couple of weeks in, we went to a Boy Scout camp. We spent the day clearing all the brush away for a place to put up our tents and lean-tos, which are three-sided shelters. Then we built the campfire for the night. It was basically all chores on that first day.

My crazy friend had a different idea of what "be prepared" meant. Back then, everything was in glass bottles. He brought a thirty-two-ounce glass Gatorade bottle. But instead of Gatorade, he filled the bottle with gasoline and brought it to Boy

Scout camp. When it came time to build the fire, he put that bottle of gasoline at the bottom of the campfire pit.

That night when they lit the fire, my crazy friend knew what was about to happen. I didn't know about his plan—Scout's honor! We were sitting twenty-five feet away from the fire pit. We were the only ones who weren't close to the fire. We were already known as the maniacs, so no one thought it was odd. When the heat of the fire finally broke the glass, the flame blew up and singed people's eyebrows. It could have been a lot worse, but thankfully it wasn't. The Scout leader grabbed us both by our collars, loaded us in his car, and drove us to the nearest pay phone. The Scout leader called my friend's father and said, "We're done with these guys. You can come pick them up."

Over thirty-five years later, I was invited to speak at Boy Scout Troop 109's Mega Eagle Court in Phoenix, at which they were honoring eight new Eagle Scouts. Needless to say, I didn't tell that story.

Growing up, I was definitely a redneck with crazy redneck friends. I was about 130 pounds in high school, so I didn't scare many people physically. I had to rely on people thinking I was crazy so they didn't mess with me. I also had good friends, such as my buddy Adam, who looked out for me. His family watched out for me, too. We did redneck things like have parties in the woods, on airboats, and in swamp buggies. We had tons of friends of all races. We all had the same thing in common—we were crazy rednecks.

When I was around eighteen, my brother Tom and I had a conversation about the example we were setting for Bryan, who was ten at the time. I said, "If we don't knock it off, Bryan's going to end up just like us. He's going to be a maniac."

I was the eighties king.

From that point forward, I went to every one of Bryan's Little League games. I was the older brother, but I did the father stuff. I announced some baseball games. I coached when he played Pop Warner football. I coached when he was in high school. From Little League through high school, I can count on one hand the total number of games he played that I missed in all those years. Our mother was usually there working the concession stand. I made a commitment to Tom and Bryan that I would be there for them like my grandfather was for me, and especially because our father wasn't there for us. He never came to any games. He hung around Florida for a few years, then he moved out to Arizona. He would call the house. If I picked up the phone and heard him say hello, I wouldn't say another word. I'd just throw the phone to my brothers. I didn't have anything to say to him.

Tom went into the Marine Corps when Bryan was a sophomore in high school, so he gave Bryan his car. Bryan was able to go to a private school on a scholarship. He went to college and graduated with honors. He's now a leader in his community and a law enforcement officer. He's married and a great father to three kids. I know that our influence while he was in school mattered. We didn't want him to be a dysfunctional mess like we were. We poured everything into him. It worked out for him. In some ways, it ended up doing more to help my life than it did for his.

ABILITY IS NOTHING WITHOUT MAKING GOOD CHOICES

I WAS DRAWN TO COACHING young people after watching my brother Bryan become influenced by my behavior when it was bad, and then watching him when I became more of a positive influence. Since my father was absent, I knew why it was important to have those positive influences in a young man's life. I might have fallen off the deep end if it weren't for friends, coaches, and the memories of my grandfather.

When Bryan went to high school, I learned how to coach high school football. The prep work was actually fun. Since I didn't spend a lot of time in school or studying when I should have been, it was somewhat ironic that I found a time when I actually enjoyed studying.

As I mentioned, Bryan was able to go to a private high school on a scholarship. The only way I was ever going to get to a place like that was by doing their electrical work, which I did end up doing. I wired the weight room for free when they built it for the players. It was a small, private Catholic high school, but it was a sports powerhouse, especially in football. It was a lot of fun to be there, because the school itself had tons of money. We had a great football field and a great baseball field for my brother to play on.

I was just hitting my stride in making steady money, but Bryan was more important. Tom and I started by making sure we were involved in Bryan's activities. I was going to be at the football games anyway, so I also went to practice every day. I was learning how to coach football from guys who were there, and they were all really, really great football coaches. It was a way for me to make friends and be a mentor to some young kids.

I love hearing from kids I coached who are now adults. I had one guy reach out to me and say, "Hey, Coach, remember me? I'm now coaching Pop Warner football. You don't know how much of an influence you were on me. It's really cool to coach my kids. Thanks for what you did for me."

Looking back on that, I realize it was not really my intention to influence all of these kids. It was a hobby and a way to be there for Bryan.

There were times when I saw kids going down the same path I did in high school. I would tell them that if they wanted to be successful beyond Pop Warner football or high school football, they had to get good grades. The schools care more about the grades than the athletics. If you're an athlete with good grades, you can write your own ticket and can go anywhere in the country.

I coached with some guys who were really good about motivating players to get good grades and were just as adamant about that as they were about the kids' athletic performance. If you didn't do your homework, you didn't practice. If you didn't practice, you didn't play. You'd better do your homework, because

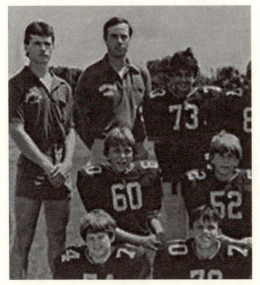

*Me on the far left
with the Cypress Lake
Hornets.*

you had to practice if you wanted to play. They stuck by those rules. If a kid was academically screwing off, they would put him on the sidelines. They didn't care if it was a starting quarterback. It sent a message to all the players: you can't skate by on just athletic ability on the team or in life. As Florida State football Coach Bobby Bowden said to a player, "Son, you have a good engine, but your hands aren't on the steering wheel."

When I was playing Pop Warner football, everybody knew Deion Sanders was going to be a superstar. Later on when I was coaching, I heard about a kid from a little migrant town who people were saying was going to be the next Deion Sanders. I said, "Listen. I played with Deion Sanders. There's one Deion Sanders."

"Wait until you see this kid," they'd tell me.

Soon enough our teams played against one another. This kid was the real deal. He was a superstar.

After the game was over, I went and said hello to the kid and told him it was a good game. This kid was all smiles. That kid, Edgerrin James, did go on to be a superstar. He went on to play at the University of Miami, and it did my heart good to see him in college. Then he went on to become the best running back in the NFL for the Indianapolis Colts after being their first-round draft pick. Then he came out here and played for the Arizona Cardinals for a few years. He was just a smart, good, young man. He was a mentor to the younger kids and talked about his experience in being mentored by the older players. I was so proud of Edgerrin James even though he wouldn't remember me to save Adam.

For every success story, there's a story about a kid with all the ability in the world who made the wrong choices. One kid who played for us was a man among boys. This kid could do anything. His mother was a single mother and drove a school bus. She was a good woman who worked very hard. All she did was support this kid and pray for him. She would work in the concession stand every night at practice. She worked the concession stand during football games on Saturday just so this kid had some structure in his life. He was the real deal. He could do anything on the football field.

Then he got in with the wrong crowd. At just sixteen, he and a twenty-two-year-old friend shot another young man, took 350 dollars off him, and left him for dead. He was sentenced to life in prison. This kid could have been the next Edgerrin James or Deion Sanders. No doubt about it. He had the athletic ability and he was smart enough. He gave up all of that potential for 350 dollars.

What's the difference between an Edgerrin James and the other kid? Both of them grew up in the same kind of neighborhood. Both of them were raised by single mothers. Edgerrin's mom worked in the school cafeteria. The other kid's mom worked as a school bus driver. They even both hung out with an older crowd. Edgerrin told *The Washington Post* that his mom "would always let me hang out with the older guys, but just as long as I didn't get into any trouble. She'd tell them, 'Take care of him, and don't let him do anything he shouldn't be doing.' I learned a lot that way, life experiences with people who used drugs, sold drugs, and did a lot of other bad stuff."

The difference is that it's all about the choices you make. The best anyone can do for his or her kids or the kids he or she mentors is to prepare them to make choices that will keep them out of trouble and on the right path.

When I think about my own life, there were probably times when my mom wondered which path I would end up going down. When I got a good job, learned a trade that kept me out of working at a fast-food place the rest of my life, and became involved in Bryan's life, I think she realized that I was going to be okay.

I haven't coached football in almost 25 years, but it still gives me gratification when the kids I coached in Pop Warner or high school football, who now have kids playing high school football, send me messages and call me Coach. They still remember me as Coach, and they will send me messages about how I influenced them in different ways. Those are bigger compliments than I deserve, because to influence somebody else's life in a positive way should be something we all want to do. There is selfishness in all of us, including me, but to have somebody say you've influenced him or her in a positive way is gratifying.

NOT EVERYONE'S JOURNEY TO SUCCESS LOOKS THE SAME

AT EIGHTEEN, I WAS MAKING minimum wage ($3.35 an hour) as an electrical apprentice. Then a guy paid me five dollars an hour. That guy was making ten or twelve dollars an hour. I thought, on the low side, ten dollars an hour is four hundred bucks a week. If I could make ten bucks an hour, I would be in high cotton. I would be over the moon. So, I started off at minimum wage, but I moved up quickly.

It was the perfect trade for me, because as an electrician, every calculation you do is algebraic. There's a lot of math involved in measuring and figuring things out. For me, it was terrific because I had to think. It wasn't like I was just digging a ditch. I had to think about what I was doing, so I was thinking and working my ass off. One of the biggest misconceptions about trade work is that it's not highly skilled. At the end of the day, I built something. I felt a sense of accomplishment. Since it was the perfect job for me, I really excelled. By the time I was twenty-four, I was the manager of the company. It was a very small company, but I was in a position in which I was managing people and learning how to be the boss. That was a pretty big accomplishment for me coming from where I did.

Once I had some money, I didn't spend a lot on clothes, but I always had a nice vehicle— within my means and used for a long time. Then when I could afford something new, I bought something new. I didn't skimp on the extras either. I had about a three-thousand-dollar stereo back then on my truck. It had 15-inch bass bins, with 300-watt amps pushing it. The bass was so strong that it vibrated the rearview mirror on the windshield. If you were sitting in the truck and hit the bass as hard as it would go, it would shake the side-view mirror and you couldn't see yourself in it.

One of the reasons I really admire TV host Mike Rowe is because he has made it his mission to promote a broader path to success. Through his organization, the mikeroweWORKS Foundation, he educates people on the trade skills gap and gives a new generation the opportunity to learn skills that are in demand.

The great thing about learning a trade is that you can do the work anywhere. You have much more freedom to be mobile. Thanks to decades of misguided guidance counselors telling kids that a four-year degree is the only way to make money, skilled trade jobs are available in practically every state.

The last US Census found that 59 percent of people were born in their current state of residence. The Midwest has the highest (70 percent) number of people who still live in their home state. One of the states with the lowest number of residents who were born there is Arizona. People go to where there's opportunity.

Moving from Florida to Arizona was one of the greatest decisions I ever made. I left Florida because I needed a change after
a painful breakup. I had no idea how fulfilling my life would be
once I got to Arizona. Being able to make that big move and
much-needed life change wouldn't have been possible if I wasn't
an electrician with the freedom to do my job anywhere. It also
enabled me to start my own business.

The opportunity to visit Arizona for the first time came from
a very unexpected source—my dad.

SOMETIMES YOU HAVE TO DIG UP SOME DIRT BEFORE BURYING THE HATCHET

AS I MENTIONED, after my parents divorced, my dad hung around Florida for a few years. We never saw him. He never came out to Bryan's games or did any of those fatherly things. He eventually moved to Arizona.

My dad said that if we ever wanted to come to Arizona, he would pay for the ticket. In 1992, I took him up on the offer because I was back to being angry and I just didn't want to be angry anymore. I decided to go out to Arizona, spend a week there, and patch things up with him.

I visited in the summertime and fell in love with Arizona. He lived in Phoenix and I stayed with him. He had a girlfriend who was terrific. She lived with him and took care of him. Unfortunately, not that much had changed with him. She was a saint, but he was still a drunk.

Early in the trip, we were in the kitchen in their house. We were talking, and the subject of my brothers and my mom came up. Some comment was made about my parents' divorce. His girlfriend interjected, "You know, there are two sides to every story. Kids don't always know the whole story in a divorce."

I said to her, "There's only one person in this room who only has one side of the story, and it's you. I know the whole story. I lived it. You've only heard it from him. I guarantee you that he's not telling you the whole story."

He had this look on his face like he had when we were kids. He was an intimidator. He was one of those guys who wanted to scare you when you were a kid. He was tiny, about five foot five. He was a little guy. But when you're a little kid, he's still a lot bigger than you. Back then, he would get this crazy-eyed look on his face. That's the look he got on his face when I challenged his story about the divorce. I looked at him and I said, "Listen, I'm not twelve anymore. That look doesn't scare me. You're going to get that look off your face or I'm going to knock you out in your own house. You're not looking at me like that anymore."

He just stood there. I said, "I'm not kidding around. I will knock you out if you don't get that look off your face." His girlfriend said, "Calm down, you guys, calm down." He just continued to stand there. I said, "You know what? I don't need this."

I went to my room and shut the door. I was supposed to leave four days later, but I called the airline and paid the extra money to leave the next morning. Then I went to sleep.

The next morning, they asked me if they could drive me to the airport. So I took the free ride to the airport. On the way, he said he wished it could have ended better. I said, "Yeah, me too." I got on the airplane and went home.

In 1994, my first marriage had ended and my brothers were off doing their own things. I went back out to Arizona again. It went better. When I eventually moved out there, I stayed with my father and his girlfriend for a while until I got my own apartment.

He didn't change. I think he just realized he couldn't intimidate me anymore. He was no longer being a bully, but he was still drinking. When he lived in Florida, he had gotten a DUI. Then he got another DUI in Arizona while I was there. My brother Tom was also living in Phoenix and working as a corrections officer. The Phoenix Police Department called us and said he was down there for a DUI. Tom said, "I'm not going to get him. I'm a freaking corrections officer. Screw him."

I had to go get him out of jail. It was always those types of incidents that made me not want to deal with him. There were some other ugly times, but we ended up being okay. By the time he got diagnosed with a terminal illness, I was past all the anger, and I saw him the day before he died.

I was lucky that my mom was supportive during those early years in Arizona. She missed me like crazy, but I would go home and visit when I could. She knew I needed a new life and that things were good for me in Arizona. I got away from a bad situation in Florida, and I ended up flourishing in Arizona. Even when I started a side career that scared the hell out of her, she was happy for me because I was doing what I wanted to do.

IF IT'S YOUR PASSION, YOU SHOULD BE WILLING TO DO IT FOR FREE

WHEN I MOVED OUT to Arizona, I jumped all-in to the culture. At some point, almost every little boy fantasizes about being a cowboy. Thanks to passion, hard work, and a lot of luck, I got to be one for a few years.

One night I met a guy named Danny. He said, "My brothers have a rodeo company."

"Who's your brother?" I asked.

"Cody Custer."

"Your brother is not Cody Custer." No joke, he almost wanted to fight because I basically called him a liar.

"Cody's my brother. You show up next weekend and you'll meet him," he said.

The next weekend I showed up at a place called WestWorld in Scottsdale, Arizona, for an event. I wasn't disappointed, and I met Danny's brothers, Cody and Jim Bob, who owned the Way Out West Company. Cody, who was inducted into the ProRodeo

Hall of Fame in 2017, is one of the founding members of the Professional Bull Riders. Jim Bob is a North American saddle bronc riding champion and Cody is a Bud Light Cup Series bull riding world champion. These guys are as good as it gets in the professional sport of bull riding.

I said to them, "I just want to learn about bull riding."

I learned everything from the ground up. Since they owned a rodeo company, my first experience was taking care of their animals. I would feed the bulls every night. It taught me the difference between the breeds of bulls. Just like any animal, bulls have personalities. If you have pets, you know that they have different personalities. It's the same thing with rodeo stock. When you're feeding them, most of them are not aggressive, even when they're in pens with other bulls. If they're protective of a herd of cows, it might be different.

I would go to the arena every night after I finished working my day job as an electrician. I would feed them eighteen bales of hay and one hundred and fifty pounds of grain. I'd break off flakes of hay and throw them on the ground. Then I'd take a bag of grain and pour it on top of the flakes of hay. The bulls would come over and eat it. They don't care who you are; they just want to get to the food. You have to watch out for them, but for the most part they're not looking for trouble.

I worked my butt off for Cody and Jim Bob, and every day I learned something. They've been involved in rodeos and bull riding since they were ten or eleven years old, and the experience of just being in their world was invaluable. They taught me about livestock, like when a bull was sick and needed medical attention. They taught me how to feed the bulls and care for them. I eventually transformed into a rodeo cowboy. I was never what they were, but I was a lot more than anybody I ever grew up with was. I traveled with the company and took bulls to rodeos. I never got paid a dime, but learned so much that I felt like I was stealing from them.

When I was feeding the bulls, I was all by myself at this place called Cave Creek Memorial Arena in Cave Creek, Arizona. At the time, the area was pretty unpopulated. I would have the arena lights on and I would sit on the tailgate of my truck and just watch those bulls eat. I felt like I had the keys to the castle.

At the time, I was broke. I was eating store-brand macaroni and cheese every night for dinner, but I was happy. I'm sure in my mind it's a lot more romantic now than it was then. I wouldn't trade those days or those friends for the world. The experience I had is worth far more than any money they could have given me.

The first time I ever got on the back of a bull, Cody was standing there and Jim Bob was the one pulling my rope. They mentored me throughout the entire process.

I was never any good at it, but I was living the dream. In the world of bull riding, I was absolutely horrible compared to everybody else. In the world of everybody else, I did something many people haven't done.

One of the best bulls I ever saw was one they owned named The Rock. This bull was beautiful. He was brown, with no horns. This bull would walk in as calm as could be. You'd climb on the back of him and he would stand there. If you wanted him to move over, you'd push him, and he would move over. He'd stand up straight for you. You'd pull your rope tight and you'd get ready to go. As soon as you nodded your head, when that gate opened, that bull would buck like he was trying to kill you.

He would jump as high in the air as he could and kick over his head and spin and try to throw you off.

The minute you hit the ground, The Rock would stop. He would back up so he didn't step on you, and walk around you, and walk out of the arena. Other bulls, all they wanted to do was get you on the ground and hook your ass. They wanted to tear you apart. The Rock was different. Bulls either buck or they don't. It's not like you force them to do anything. They're good at it or they're not good at it. They have fun with it or they don't have fun with it. The good ones like The Rock are just fun to watch.

I did some amateur bull riding. I rode for quite a while before I got injured. This happened before everybody started wearing protective helmets. I just wore a protective vest. It helped me out since I got jumped on a couple of times. That vest saved my vital organs.

For me, the draw to bull riding was the mental challenge, not the physical challenge. It was terrifying and exhilarating at the same time. I got on one of those bulls and thought, "I just want to live," as dumb as that sounds. At the same time, when I not only survived but also made the whistle by staying on for eight seconds and maybe winning some money, I felt ten feet tall and bulletproof. I felt like I'd accomplished something. Now when I look back at the video, it's just this little bull that couldn't hurt anybody. We called them dinks. It didn't matter, because it felt like I was on top of the world.

We would hang out at an iconic bar called Mr. Lucky's Night Club. Its sign is a joker from a playing card. The sign was a Phoenix landmark, but unfortunately, the bar is closed now. An incredible musician named J. David Sloan owned the bar. He was friends with Waylon Jennings, who made appearances there. David knew everybody in the music business. He had a great band called Western Bread that played in his bar. David built a bull-riding arena on the outside of the bar that was really popular. They would buck bulls and practice on Wednesday night. Then the bar would have open bull riding with good bull riders on Friday night. Saturday night was for the novice bull riders. There would be 500 to 1,000 people there every Friday and Saturday night.

There would be guys lined up to get in. I was riding but wasn't doing really well since I was still learning. They needed somebody to announce a charity event they had one weekend, so I volunteered to do it. I caught on to announcing because I used to announce baseball games. It was fun, and I ended up being the regular announcer at this bar.

We had a good group there. I was the bull-riding announcer. My roommate was the bull rider, and my best friend was the bull-fighter. There would be three rounds of riding, then the riders would take the payout and the crowd would cheer. We'd stand in the arena after the rounds of bull riding and there would be girls (they called them "buckle bunnies") lined up at the fence who wanted to talk to us, especially if they were on vacation from out of town. The loved the idea of meeting a cowboy, and people lined up at the fence wanting to take pictures with us.

We were in this tiny world, but in that world, we were kind of a big deal. I never lost perspective, because I knew I sucked at it. When you learn how to ride bulls from a guy who is a world champion and has ridden the baddest bulls on the planet, you know you suck. It's all perspective.

The logo for the Way Out West Company was "WOW" in big gold letters. I had achieved this childhood fantasy of being

With my bullriding heroes, from left: Luke Kraut, me, Cody Custer, Dave Cicogni

a cowboy and it was cool to be able to go home for a visit with all of this new knowledge and experience. One night some old friends and I went out to a local country bar. I was wearing my buckle with my name on it that I had gotten from the rodeo company. I was a real cowboy in a country bar in a beach town with a lot of posers. We were hanging out. I wasn't a big drinker and definitely didn't drink much beer. These three girls came walking in, and they were all really good-looking. There was one blonde girl who was just gorgeous. This whole group of girls stood out in a bar like that.

I was with a few of my former coworkers and some of my childhood friends. There was about a group of six or seven of us. A song came on and they all went out and danced with their girls. I was standing there all by myself. The waitress brought me a beer and said it was from the blonde girl. I looked over where the three girls were, and the blonde girl waved. I walked over and thanked her for the beer. All my buddies came over and started giving it to me about going over to the girls as soon as they walked away. I said, "I didn't go anywhere. She bought me the beer. I don't even drink this beer."

The blonde said, "Yep, I bought him the beer."

It was at that moment that my friends realized the difference between a real cowboy and a poser.

Of course, it wasn't all free drinks and pretty girls wanting pictures. I broke my right ankle on the inside, and then my anklebone was broken off. I also broke my fibula and the outside bone on my right leg. A bull jumped on the outside of my right leg, and it broke off the bone on the inside. I got them all screwed back together. Then a few months later, I got on a practice bull for a rodeo exhibition for the Jewish Funeral Directors of America. That bull jumped on me and broke the very same bones. All the metal inside was bent, so the doctors had to take it all out and then put all the metal back in again. The next time I broke my foot. Then I broke my shoulder. All of the breaks were in the span of a year. I was always hurt. I was afraid, and one thing you can't be is too afraid to perform. Being afraid kind of pissed me off and ultimately was one of the reasons I quit.

On Monday through Friday, I would be working but thinking about getting on a bull. Then Saturday and Sunday would come, and I would be sweating about getting on and breaking something else. One Saturday, I was especially nervous. I walked away out of the other riders' sight. I hadn't prayed in years and I was embarrassed. I prayed to God that I just wouldn't be afraid anymore. I didn't care what happened after I got off; I just didn't want to be afraid. During the time it took to walk to get on my bull, relief came over me and that fear was gone. I got on the bull and had one of the best rides of my career.

When I got off the bull and jumped over the chute, my Christian roommate, was standing there said, "What the heck got into you?"

It was kind of a compliment because he wasn't carrying me to the truck for a change. I said, "I gotta find a church." This shocked him even more than watching me ride my bull, because he knew I was living a rowdy life.

The other reason I quit was that I didn't like missing work because of injuries.

The greatest lesson I learned from my time in bull riding was that I will always regret the things I didn't do more than the things I did. That's one of the reasons it was easy to load up my truck with everything I owned, and all the money I had in my pocket, and move to Arizona. That was in 1995. Look where I am now. None of this would have happened if I didn't get in that truck and make the move.

The other lesson is you should be willing to do what you love for free. Do whatever it takes to pay the bills. If you're lucky enough and you're good enough, doing what you love will earn you a living. Even if it doesn't, you get to do what you love.

I spent seven days a week driving twenty miles from my house to load eighteen bales of hay and one hundred and fifty pounds of grain into the back of my truck, and fill water troughs for about forty bulls for years. I'd truck them across town and across the state. I didn't get paid a dime, but I didn't want to get paid. I wanted the experience.

The best songwriters, the best writers, and the best artists are people who never in a million years thought anybody would listen to their songs, read their books, or see their art. They did it because they loved it. It wasn't about becoming famous. Pursuing their passion wasn't about getting recognition but about doing what they loved. It made them feel like they were accomplishing something.

If I had walked into that event with Cody and Jim Bob Custer at twenty-seven years old and said, "I'm here to be a world champion bull rider," they would have sent me down the road. Instead, I volunteered to do anything that would put me in a position to gain valuable experience. There are a lot of people in the rodeo business—and any business—who would say, "I would never do that grunt work for free." I would say to them, "That's you. Maybe you grew up in this business and you know what you're doing." I learned everything I know from these guys and on their dime with their equipment, so to speak. I got everything I wanted. Doing the grunt work was my way into a business that I loved.

REMEMBER THOSE WHO SACRIFICED FOR YOUR FREEDOMS

MY BROTHER TOM was a lot less vocal than I am. You learned about Tom by watching him rather than hearing him. I now make a living in which people listen to what I say. They don't necessarily know me, but they might take stock in the words I say. Tom was someone who didn't say much, but the people around him learned a lot by the way he behaved.

Tom joined the Marines in 1990. He was stationed in California, got out in 1994, and moved to Arizona. He worked at the state prison in Florence, Arizona. Then I moved there, and we lived together.

Eventually he met his wife, who had three small children whom he adopted. In order to care for them properly, he decided to go back into the military and join the Army. He loved it and wanted it to be his career. He decided to join the Army because they gave him a choice of duty stations. He had already been deployed once as a Marine, and he was afraid if he got deployed

When Tom (left) and I lived together in Arizona in 1996.

again, his wife would be stuck on a Marine base somewhere in the middle of nowhere with three kids. He chose Fort Carson in Colorado because her family lived five minutes from there. He loved the Marines, but he chose the Army the second time around because it was better for his family.

When 9/11 happened, he was one of my first calls.

"What's happening?" I asked him.

"We're going. I just don't know when. We don't know; obviously something's going to happen and we're going to be in it," he said without hesitation.

The invasion happened in March of 2003. He wasn't part of the first invasion. His unit followed the invasion into Baghdad.

All the commentators and naysayers said the Republican Guard of Saddam Hussein was battle-hardened and tested. They waxed on about it being Saddam's terrain. They said the coalition forces could expect tens of thousands of casualties in the push to Baghdad. Then our forces cut through those guys like they were butter. They strolled into Baghdad.

That's when I first noticed the divide in our country between the media elite and the rest of us who actually know people in the military. It's not that the media elite are unintelligent. They just never meet or talk with the people who actually do the work. They want to interview the generals. I want to interview the generals, but I also want to interview the sergeants. The media would have known what was going to happen if they had interviewed the guys like my brother who were in the first Gulf War. He would have said, "You think the Republican Guard is going to beat us? Look at our equipment. Look at who our guys are."

He was with the Eagle Troop of the 2nd Squadron, 3rd Armored Cavalry Regiment out of Fort Carson, which later moved to Fort Hood. The regiment was called the Brave Rifles, and its motto written by Wilfred Scott was "Brave rifles! Veterans! You have been baptized in fire and blood and have come out steel." General H.R. McMaster led the regiment in the first Gulf War.

Tom was in a Bradley armored vehicle unit. When he and his fellow squadron members moved into the Sunni triangle, they were first in a town called Ramadi. His platoon leader, KC Hughes, was actually younger than Tom. Tom was thirty-four. KC was in his late twenties. They had come up with an idea that night in Ramadi. They would jump in a car dressed in civilian clothes and drive around the city. They would look for young men with rifles, so they would know that a military stronghold was hidden in that place. Then they would go back and devise a plan to either hit it that night or hit it the next day to get rid of the militants in Ramadi.

It worked so well that when they locked down Ramadi, they moved my brother's platoon into Fallujah on Memorial Day weekend. In Fallujah, they would have attacks at night. There were three or four freeway entrances into the city. They didn't know if the attacks were coming from within the city or if people were coming into the city, hitting it, and moving out. They came up with a plan that they would shut down the freeways at night and check every vehicle coming into the city at all three or four checkpoints. If the attacks stopped, they would know that the attackers were coming from outside the city. If the attacks continued, that meant they were coming from inside the city and they had to start looking there.

On Memorial Day in Iraq, Tom and Sergeant Mike Quinn from Tampa, Florida, were outside the city and checking vehicles as they came into the city. A vehicle pulled up and opened fire on my brother and Mike. Mike was killed instantly. Tom was shot in the legs. Tom pulled himself to safety and took out the initial attackers. He shot the guys and took them out by himself. Their platoon was ambushed. There were people waiting in the building close to them. In the firefight, nine other guys were wounded, including KC, who was shot through the collarbone in the back.

They had a critical response team, another group of Bradleys and their fighting vehicles that were waiting to help in an emergency. They called in that team to come and assist, and they called for ambulances and helicopters for the wounded. The other Bradleys were blacked out and racing down the freeway. The first helicopter started taking small-arms fire as it was trying to land in the landing zone. Instead of the pilot going to the

48

landing there, he almost landed on top of one of the Bradleys and crashed. It was just chaos.

The next helicopter that landed took the pilot and crew from the crashed helicopter instead of my brother or the other wounded guys. During the time when they were waiting for a third helicopter to show up, Tom was cracking jokes and calming everybody down, since he was ten years older than most of the guys around him. He wanted to look out for the younger guys. He was also doing triage and everything else with them. When another ambulance helicopter finally showed up, they took my brother out first because he was bleeding so badly. He had gotten hit in the femoral artery in his leg, and there was no stopping the bleeding. He bled out and died before he got to the hospital.

The Tuesday after Memorial Day, I got a call from a number in Florida that I didn't know. With a mother who is older, a brother who is deployed, and a brother who is a cop, I knew it was probably not good news. I answered it and a voice said, "Hey, my name is Ken. I work with your mom. I don't know how to tell you this, but your brother Tom was killed in Iraq."

The first thing I said was, "How is my mom?"

"She's being taken care of. We are with her. The military is still with her. She's okay. Your brother is on his way," he said.

"Okay, thanks," I said, and hung up the phone. Then I called my brother Bryan, who was driving from work to my mother.

My church paid for my family's plane tickets to go to Florida the next day. At six o'clock the next morning, I was on a flight going home.

In October of 2017, the media became focused on President Trump's outreach to Gold Star families. In a press briefing from the White House, General John Kelly, who lost a son in combat, described what happens after a soldier dies in combat:

> Most Americans don't know what happens when we lose one of our soldiers, sailors, airmen, Marines, or Coast Guardsmen in combat. So let me tell you what happens.
>
> Their buddies wrap them up in whatever passes as a shroud, puts them on a helicopter as a routine and send them home. Their first stop along the way is when they're packed in ice, typically at the airhead and then they're flown to, usually Europe, where they're then packed in ice again and flown to Dover Air Force Base, where Dover takes care of the remains, embalms them, meticulously dresses them in their uniform with the—medals that they've earned, the emblems of their service, and then puts them on another airplane linked up with a casualty officer escort that takes them home.
>
> A very, very good movie to watch, if you haven't ever seen it, is Taking Chance....Chance Phelps was killed under my command right next to me, and it's worth seeing that if you've never seen it.
>
> So that's the process. While that's happening, a casualty officer typically goes to the home very early in the morning and waits for the first lights to come on. And then he knocks on the door; typically a mom and dad will answer, [or] a wife. And if there is a wife, this is happening in two different places; if the parents are divorced, three different places. And the casualty officer proceeds to break the heart of a family member and stays with that family until—well, for a long, long time, even after the internment. So that's what happens.
>
> Who are these young men and women? They are the best one percent this country produces.

There wasn't an Army post near my mom, so a team from MacDill Air Force Base in Tampa showed up at my mother's office and notified her in her office. Then they called my brother at work. I had been on a short-term mission trip on the Navajo reservation with my church over Memorial Day weekend. The first call I got that Tuesday morning was the call from Ken.

I flew to Florida on Wednesday. On Thursday, there was a press conference. My brother was so distraught about having to talk. Bryan is this big, burly cop. He loved Tom so much, as we all did. Of course, being the big brother, instead of consoling him, I made fun of him about it the whole time. We were driving to the press conference and he kept saying, "I'm not talking."

I told him that I would talk and to not worry about it. Just to mess with him and lighten the situation, I said, "Wouldn't it be funny if we pulled in here and there were satellite trucks?"

He turned white and said, "That's not funny."

"Bryan, come on. It's Fort Myers. There's just going to be a TV camera from the local TV station. There will be a reporter from the newspaper and someone taking our picture. It's not going to be a big deal," I told him.

We pulled around the corner to the hospital where my mom worked. Their PR department had set this up in the atrium of the hospital. There were satellite trucks everywhere. There were tons of cameras. It was like paparazzi. Bryan actually looked at me like I had known this was going to happen. I said, "Dude, I had an idea. I was joking. I had no idea this was going to be this big of a deal."

We walked into the hospital and we literally had to run to the bathroom to compose ourselves before we could start the press conference.

I've never written a speech in my life. Even now, with the opportunities I've had to speak in public, I've never written a speech. At that moment before the press conference, and with any public speaking I've done since, it has always been important to me to speak from the heart. All I cared about was giving the people who were there a picture of who Tom was, what we thought of him, and what he thought his duty was.

I wrote three bullet points down to make sure I stayed on track. I wanted to talk about how proud we were of him and the men and women he had served with, and of the other men and women who were serving. I also wanted to make sure we mentioned that my brother had stood with the president and his mission, because there had been such a backlash about what was going on regarding the war at that time. By the time I reached the end of my remarks, a crowd of a few hundred people had gathered to hear us.

At the end, I talked about the protesters. I said, "My brother believed in your right to protest. The only thing that we would ask as a family would be to remember that it's because of men and women like him, that you have the freedom to protest in safety."

When I was done, there was a round of applause from the people in that hospital atrium, including the people in some of the hospital rooms who had come out. It scared us. It was so loud that I looked at Bryan and we were startled. At that moment, I realized my brother's story had connected with people and I owed it to him to share it.

After the memorial in Fort Myers, I flew to Colorado for the funeral on June 7. My brother was buried near Fort Carson, rather than Arlington National Cemetery, because that's the Army installation where his wife and the boys were. It was still early in the war, so the entire command staff from Fort Carson was there. The wives and girlfriends of my brother's platoon mates were also there. Every one of those people knew Tom. They were a mess because everybody loved him. But at the same time, in their hearts, they were so thankful that it wasn't their soldier.

As I sat there before officiating and speaking at Tom's funeral, I kept looking around the room. The command staff were distraught. The wives, girlfriends, and kids were distraught. Then I looked at my family. I looked at Tom's wife and his three young kids. I looked at my mom and my brother Bryan. I thought, "How am I going to say anything that means anything to anybody?"

When it was time for me speak, I said, "I understand how sad you are about Tom. We also understand how thankful you are that it's not your soldier who died. We want you to know that Tom would feel that way, too. Tom wouldn't have it any other way. Tom would have gladly been the one to sacrifice his life so that your soldier could live."

After the service, music by Hootie and the Blowfish was played because it was Tom's favorite band. So, Hootie was playing and people were crying. I was on the stage with my buddy and pastor, Robb. He leaned over to me and whispered, "I've never shared the gospel and then been followed by Hootie and the Blowfish."

We couldn't help but laugh. Of course, my mom was in the audience and caught my eye and gave me that look women give when you're misbehaving.

Many years later, I had the opportunity to meet Darius Rucker, the lead singer of Hootie and the Blowfish. I'm also a huge fan of his solo work. I told him about playing his music at my brother's funeral. I could tell he was touched, but I know it probably meant more for me to tell the story than it meant for him to hear it. I told him I couldn't hear one of his songs and not think about my brother. Every time I hear a Hootie and the Blowfish song, it's great because I feel like my brother Tom is sitting right next to me.

When I got back to Phoenix, I walked into my office, and on my desk was a letter from Tom postmarked the day he was killed. He mailed that letter in the afternoon and got killed that night. Just a few weeks earlier, I had sent Tom a letter. I told him that he and the other soldiers there were heroes. I wrote that what they were doing was good for America. I wrote how much I honored what he was doing. My letter might have been the last piece of home and family he saw. His letter to me is the most important thing I have. He wrote everything I had said at the press conference. It just confirmed for me that I needed to keep telling his story. I keep that letter in my safe. That's how much it means.

After the funeral, I talked to a guy who had been there with Tom when he died. He said, "Tom's first instinct was to protect us, because he opened fire and took out the initial attackers. Then he was cracking jokes. The last thing he did when they loaded him up on the ambulance was crack jokes. He was always looking out for us."

In 2008, five years after Tom died, I got a phone call from a guy who had known Tom. He said, "Hey, my name is Bruce. I was a freshman in high school when Tom was a senior. Everybody used to pick on the freshmen. Tom always looked out for us. He always told us how great we were going to be."

Tom was the quarterback of the high school football team and hung out with the offensive linemen because he didn't want to be the center of attention. It wasn't fake humility. He really just wanted to be a part of the team. He didn't want attention. He didn't want to speak. He didn't want to be noticed. He just wanted to do his job.

Bruce and some other local business owners in Fort Myers paid for and got permission to change the name of the Cypress Lake High School football stadium to the Thomas Broomhead Memorial Stadium. They paid for the monument out in front of the stadium, and they paid for the scoreboard signage.

How incredible that in 1987, kids thought the exact same thing about an eighteen-year-old on a high school football field, who in 2003, members of the military also thought about him on the battlefield in Iraq. He always looked out for everybody else. I'm just amazed at who he was.

My drive and commitment to issues that affect veterans, like the mess the Veterans Administration hospitals have become, comes from the fact that if Tom had survived that night, he would have been permanently changed. I don't know to what degree or severity. He would have been permanently changed because he was so dedicated to the people around him. If we don't understand the camaraderie and the brotherhood of the military, we're doing all of our service members a disservice.

The country has done such a disservice to these men and women by allowing fraud and corruption to exist within the VA. We bring people home from battle and we don't help them cope, because we don't understand the love they share and the loss they feel. Every single person who served with my brother lost two brothers that night. Not just Tom but also

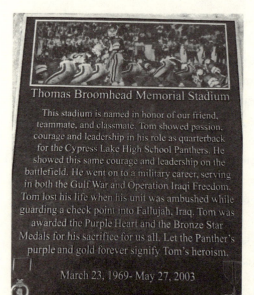

Thomas Broomhead Memorial Stadium

This stadium is named in honor of our friend, teammate, and classmate. Tom showed passion, courage and leadership in his role as quarterback for the Cypress Lake High School Panthers. He showed this same courage and leadership on the battlefield. He went on to a military career, serving in both the Gulf War and Operation Iraqi Freedom. Tom lost his life when his unit was ambushed while guarding a check point into Fallujah, Iraq. Tom was awarded the Purple Heart and the Bronze Star Medals for his sacrifice for us all. Let the Panther's purple and gold forever signify Tom's heroism.

March 23, 1969- May 27, 2003

Plaque and scoreboard on the field at Cypress Lake High School in Fort Myers dedicated to my brother Tom.

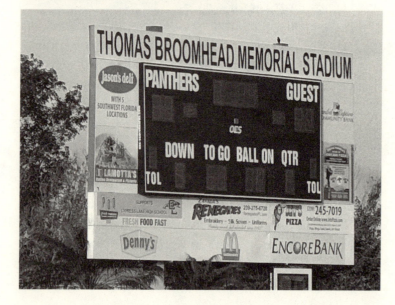

Sergeant Mike Quinn. If we don't recognize that they are as distraught as we are, we're not properly honoring what they do. I am driven to be a veteran's advocate because I can picture Tom as a survivor and what he would have done.

I didn't work for over a month after Tom died. My mother and Bryan also didn't work for a month. But my brother's platoon got up the next morning after losing eleven men, grieved for a short time, picked up their weapons, and went back to work.

There are so many people in the military who just do their job every day. They're not asking for anything in return. Tom was a silent hero. Recognizing his dedication and service matters to me. I wrote this book because I want readers, including future generations of my family, to know who he was. We feel like we've lost so much because God blessed us with so much.

Be Respectful, but Be Honest

A WEEK OR SO AFTER the funeral, I made my first call to a local talk radio show on KFYI, the most popular talk radio station in Phoenix. The host, Bruce Jacobs, put me on the air a couple of times. Then people wanted to hear Tom's whole story, and Bruce got me speaking around town so I could share it.

In 2004 and 2005, the anti-war protestors were coming out of the woodwork and Cindy Sheehan was a household name. Her son, Casey, was killed in action in Iraq on April 4, 2004. She became the go-to for the anti-war side. I didn't debate her one-on-one, but I was called to counter her points and other things she had said many times.

As many people have pointed out, there were more deaths in Afghanistan under President Barack Obama than there were under President George Bush. It's not like things changed a whole lot, but the protestors sure went away once Bush did. Even those who may have been against the war, especially libertarians, saw the hypocrisy on the left and in the media once Obama took office.

After Tom's death, I traveled with a group called Gold Star Families United. It was a group mostly of parents, but there were some like me with siblings who had died in the war on terrorism.

We would travel to events and speak as a group. There were about thirty of us, and at each event, five or six of us would speak. Speaking came really easily to me, because I was talking about Tom and speaking from the heart.

When our group of Gold Star families traveled, we never talked about politics. There was camaraderie because of our shared grief and loss. We talked about the loved ones we'd lost. We talked about the good times with them. There was an instant connection because we all understood how the loss impacted us in the simplest ways. We really took comfort in being together. We didn't spend a lot of time on the political side of what was happening with the war.

The atmosphere was bizarre at times, because I really respect all parents and family members who have lost someone, even Cindy Sheehan. We were all mindful of the fact that she was also a Gold Star mother and she was suffering the same kind of loss that we were. Gold Star Families United made a good effort to never insult her publicly, even though we disagreed. It was very noble of the group, because Cindy Sheehan said some really off-the-wall things. It didn't stop after the Bush years either. In 2012, the federal government sued her for not paying taxes. She said, "I feel like I gave my son to this country in an illegal and immoral war. I'll never get him back. And, so, if they can give me my son back, then I'll pay my taxes. And that's not going to happen."

My intention was to always be respectful to Sheehan, but for me the gloves came off when she made a comment about the mothers who supported the war. About these mothers, Sheehan wrote on Huffington Post, "I am starting to lose a little compassion for them. I know they have been as brainwashed as the rest of America, but they know the pain and heartache and they should not wish it on another. However, I still feel their pain so acutely and pray for these 'continue the murder and mayhem' moms to see the light."

I thought, "Well, now that you're going to insult my mom, all bets are off." That's when I broke from the group and said whatever I wanted to say.

I've seen protestors do some awful things, and I'll never forget that Sheehan was their poster girl. She led an anti-war protest in DC, and we did a counterevent at the National Mall the next day called the Rally to Honor Military Families. I got to speak, and it was one of the most moving moments of my life. I was standing with my back to the Capitol and looking out at the Washington Monument. Off in the distance was the Lincoln Memorial, and I thought, "That's where MLK spoke."

I was on a stage looking at it and getting ready to speak. I thought, "Nobody is going to remember my speech for eternity, but wow this is pretty cool." I remember that moment, thinking how does this redneck kid from the middle of nowhere stand at the National Mall and give a speech about anything? It was very, very moving to me. It was a moment in my life I'll never forget, because again, it wasn't anything that I had ever done that got me there. I will never lose sight of the fact that if it weren't for my brother's sacrifice, I wouldn't be where I am. I would also happily give it all up for ten more minutes with him.

During that trip to DC, the anti-war crowd put up a memorial of its own. They attached pictures of service members who

Speaking on the National Mall in Washington D.C. with Gold Star Families United in 2004.

had died. There were several related to those in our group. The anti-war group allowed our families to remove their family members' pictures from the anti-war memorial. I thought that was a very civil thing for the anti-war group to do.

However, when the parents went to take their loved ones' pictures down, protestors were screaming the vilest language and spitting on them. There was a woman named M.J. Kesterson. I'll never forget her. Her son had been a helicopter pilot and was killed. These protestors were screaming in her face, and she looked at one of the protestors and said, "I just want my son's picture."

M.J. was dumbfounded. She just wanted to get her late son's photo, and these evil, vile people were screaming at her.

If anybody on our side of that argument had screamed at Cindy Sheehan like that, their side would have come even more unhinged. That's when I knew there were two sets of rules and a double standard in play. We had to be on our best behavior, but they could behave any way they wanted. It was disturbing to me.

Sheehan fed the media's anti-war, anti-Bush narrative. Reporters would ask her softball questions and let her hit them out of the park. The media was much more skeptical of us.

After three or four of us from the Gold Star families spoke on the National Mall, we went back to a hotel ballroom, where the media was able to ask any one of us questions individually.

One of the reporters asked me, "When is it enough loss? When is that time? When is the cost too high?"

On the airplane from Phoenix to DC, I read one of my favorite books, *Strength to Love*, by Martin Luther King Jr. It's a small book, a compilation of sermons he gave at black churches in the South. I was so moved by the civil rights movement, his vision of Christian duty, and by how he saw it as his duty as a black man to fight for equality and civil disobedience. His sermons were so moving that he inspired people who just wanted to ride the bus and sit where they wanted to fight for equality on all fronts. It was just such a simple act and yet, they were willing to lose their houses and jobs and take beatings in some cases. All of that chaos was just to get some semblance of equality. He was speaking out to encourage all these church congregations.

Several members of the media at that ballroom in DC were black. I didn't know how my comments were going to be perceived by them, but I talked about Martin Luther King Jr.'s message and mission. I said, "I read the book *Strength to Love*, and there's a quote in the book that stuck with me. I'm paraphrasing, but he basically said, 'we will never gain the respect of white people in the South or anywhere else if we are willing to trade our children's future for our own personal comfort and safety.'"

I said, "Would anybody here dare to ask Martin Luther King Jr. during those times, when is enough enough? When are enough homes lost? When are enough jobs lost? The ridicule, the police brutality, when is that enough? When are you just going to sit on the bus where you're told? Nobody would have ever dared to ask him that, and if they'd said enough is enough, where would we be?"

I continued, "I don't know when enough is enough. How do you ask me that question? It's over when it's over." I waited to see if I was going to get a really negative reaction, but it seemed like a few of them nodded a little bit and understood my connection to that story.

In general, the media was very skeptical about our involvement and support of the president and the war on terrorism. They would ask questions like "How many deaths are enough?" and "How much blood has to be spilled?"

Cindy Sheehan never faced that kind of criticism. She was treated with kid gloves. She could say the most outlandish things. She could call mothers who supported the war "murder and mayhem moms" and no one would say, "How do you think a mother who has lost a son and cries every day feels when she hears you say that?"

If we had said something like that about her, the media would have eviscerated us. There was a huge double standard, and it's because of a difference in political ideology.

The majority of the members of the media think it's the government's job to care for its people, not to protect its people.

There are ideological differences because most of them are on the left. I think it's the government's job to make sure that the borders are secure. Let the government make sure that we're protected militarily. Let's have the strongest military possible. Let's make sure the roads are good. That's the government's job, the freeways and the roads. Let the local governments figure out how to take care of their people. Let the local governments educate.

The media and academia's mentality is that the bulk of taxes should go to support the poor and the entitlement programs. Anything that takes away from those programs, such as the military and defense (the primary function of the government), is looked at by them as the removal of resources from their programs.

There's been an ongoing animosity between academia and the military since the 1960s when the horrible killing of four students at Kent State University happened. Even today, there are state-run universities that don't want military recruiters on their campuses.

When service members come back and use funds provided by the GI Bill to go to college, they're faced with people who have no idea what they've been through. They are there to get an education and move on with their lives. Instead, many of them face this anti-military atmosphere on college campuses.

Prior to the Rally to Honor Military Families, I called in to Sean Hannity's show to talk about these issues, because I was really deep into it. Sean and I developed quite a rapport. He came to Phoenix for a visit, and I got to meet him for the first time. He's always been very friendly and very good to me.

Sean knew that my family's story was as impactful as Cindy Sheehan's story. Since I supported the war on terrorism, he let me tell my story because I had as much to offer as she did.

A liberal radio host who didn't know my family's story also interviewed me. This host was talking about Sheehan having the right to speak out. He said that because of the sacrifice of her family, when she speaks, whether you agree or not, you should just shut up and listen.

I said, "So, if somebody from the other side was talking to you, since you haven't lost anybody in the war, you should just shut up and listen to them? Well, my brother died on Memorial Day of 2003. Are you going to shut up and listen to me?"

The host was dumbfounded for a couple of seconds, because I had boxed him into a corner. In the liberal media's world, Cindy Sheehan gets to say what she wants without honest criticism, but those who have had the same loss and a different political view don't.

At an event in Phoenix, there was a Vietnam veteran protesting the war, which was a rare instance. Generally, Vietnam veterans have been very good to my family, but this guy was a protestor and talking to the media. He turned to me and said, "There's no difference between your brother and the terrorists who are over there. They both have guns and they're both using them."

He was clearly trying to say something to get me riled up. I didn't respond to him then. I waited until everything died down, and I went to have a one-on-one conversation with him. Not only was he a Vietnam veteran, but he had also seen combat. Right away, I backed off, because I'd never been in combat. I decided not to blast this guy, because he deserved my respect. However, I still wanted to talk to him and make my case for why I thought he was wrong in making that comparison.

I said, "The difference is that my brother fought because he loved America, not because he hated Muslims. The terrorists don't fight because they love their country. The terrorists are fighting because they hate America. They're fighting for hate. They hate the Western world. They hate us. They hate freedom. My brother wrote in his letters home that he thought he was giving the Iraqi people a chance at freedom. He thought he was doing a peaceful, good thing for people who had been oppressed by Saddam Hussein. That's the difference."

In the end, this guy was such a nice guy and I didn't change his mind about America being at war, but he apologized for comparing my brother to a terrorist. When people are in a mob or large group discussing war, there are the pro-troops and anti-war sides. Both sides get loud and proud. But individually, when we talk to each other, we find out we're not that far off on what we want. We're just off on what we think is going to get us there.

Many times people don't see the dichotomy that they create. That on one hand they are always on the side of angels until proven differently, and that on the other hand, the opposing side is always on the side of the devil. That's human nature to a certain extent.

I ended up having a really nice, respectful conversation with this Vietnam veteran, and he shook my hand and we walked away peacefully. In many situations, that's the best you're ever going to get, and it needs to happen a lot more often.

HAVE A GOOD MENTOR

I AM FORTUNATE to have had several good mentors in my personal life. My grandfather taught me what it meant to be a man and a provider. My mom worked three jobs, seven days a week. She never made excuses. I'm proud that I got my work ethic from her and my grandfather. My grandfather laid the foundation and my mother built the house. My brothers, Tom and Bryan, taught me about being a good, honest person through their actions.

In my career, I've also had some important relationships that have given me confidence and caused me to be introspective. After calling in to a few radio shows to talk about Tom's story, I was asked to be a guest and co-host on a smaller station in Phoenix in 2004. We did the show for three hours in an afternoon. I can't remember one thing we talked about, to be honest with you, but it was fun. After the show, the station manager said, "Man, you're good at this. You want to do a show?"

"I work on weekdays, but I can do it on the weekends," I said.

"Just come in on Saturday and I'll give you a two-hour show. We can't pay you, but we normally sell that time, so I won't charge you either."

So, I went out and bought headphones and showed up on Saturday morning and prepped, not knowing what I was really getting into. When I got to the studio, the board operator said to me, "All right, you've got a floating break at about fifteen and forty-five. You've got a hard break at the bottom of the hour and at the top of the hour. Also, you've got to hit the post at 59:50, because we go to national news."

I looked at him and said, "I don't know what a floating break is, I don't know what a hard break is, and I don't know what the post is or how to hit it."

He said, "Are you kidding me?"

I said, "I have never done this before."

This guy literally had to talk me through the clock for two hours. During the first show, all I did was worry about when I had to go to commercial. Was I talking too long? Was I cutting off too soon? I'm sure it was a disaster, and I hope there's no recording of it anywhere. Going into it, I was worried about the content when I should have been worried about the timing.

During that first two-hour show at the small station in Phoenix, I would take calls. The station had a very loyal fan base. Callers aren't worried about timing at all, so that made it even trickier. They're not going to understand why you have to cut them off for a hard break for commercials. They're just going to think you're a jerk. People would e-mail me, and that was my introduction to the haters. I got some pretty evil e-mails. It's just the nature of the game. You consider the source and move on.

I started off doing just the Saturday show, and then added a three-hour show on Sunday afternoon. I was still in training and basically just filling up unused sponsored time.

Pretty soon I started filling in for Bruce Jacobs, the host at KFYI who did the shift from five o'clock to eight o'clock in the morning.

I filled in for him when he would go on vacation and then for two weeks around Christmas. I was also still doing my Saturday and Sunday shows. So, there were times when I was on the air for twenty days straight and still doing my day job running an electrical company.

When Bruce Jacobs left the station in 2009, they gave me that early-morning show, but gave the morning drive-host, Barry Young, an extra hour. So, I did five o'clock to seven o'clock in the morning. Then, in early 2010, the afternoon guy at KFYI, former Congressman J.D. Hayworth, ran against John McCain for the Senate in the primary. They gave me that slot, and I was the afternoon-drive host for a little over four years. When Barry Young retired after twenty-seven years, they gave me the morning-drive slot, which became six o'clock in the morning to ten o'clock in the morning. Almost six years to the day I made my first call in to that show, I ended up in that time slot.

By mid-2010, I was doing three, later four, hours of radio per day and all the other work that goes along with it. I had to start phasing out my electrical business. No one is more surprised than me that I ended up having a career in broadcasting. Even though I enjoyed what I was doing and didn't have a problem speaking for a couple of hours a day, not a day went by when I didn't expect it to end.

When I had two years or so of full-time experience in talk radio and was still on the air in the afternoons, I got an e-mail from an AOL e-mail address. I truly didn't think it was legit. I mean, AOL?

It basically said, "I'm a talent development guy for Glenn Beck. I've been listening to your show online and wondered if you'd be interested in filling in for Glenn one day."

I couldn't help but laugh. I was vacationing with my mom, and when I read her the e-mail, she was just over the moon. She loves Glenn. I said, "This can't be real. This is some guy who says, 'I can get a connection. Just get me a tape and I'll get it to the right person.' Then he later expects something from you."

But it was legit. In 2012, I got to guest host my first show for Glenn for two days during the Christmas season. Afterward, Glenn and I would talk on the phone about how the show went and he'd coach me up a little bit.

I didn't get to meet Glenn until 2013, when he was in Phoenix doing his show. The event organizer wanted me to introduce Glenn on stage because he thought that since I filled in for him, I must have met him. Before the event, we met up in one of the KFYI studios, because he would do his show from there since he was traveling.

He said, "I'm hearing some good things about you. How's it going?"

Like a dope, I couldn't do anything else except tell the truth. I said, "Glenn, I'm in so far over my head. I have no idea what I'm doing. I had a boss who would tell me one week at a meeting to do one thing every time. Then two weeks later in a meeting, he would say, 'Don't ever do that same thing again.' I'm writing stuff down and I'm doing exactly what he tells me to do. I'm keeping it all in one notepad so I can go back to my notes. None of it makes sense to me."

Glenn said, "Come to Dallas and watch my people."

I went to Dallas and shadowed him for three days. It was a great experience to see his people, all at the top of their field.

If you gave me a set of blueprints, I could roll them out on the table right now and by looking at the blueprints, tell you where you're going to have issues during construction because I've been doing that my whole life. When it comes to radio, I don't know when I'm good and I don't know when I'm bad.

It's easier with a live crowd. I can be speaking and know when I'm being funny or entertaining. I know when I'm telling a story about my mom or my brother and see people tear up. I know when I'm connecting with them. On the radio, I'm in a soundproof room. I have on headphones, and I sit in front of a microphone and talk to myself. Early on in my broadcasting career, I felt like I was getting caught singing in my truck.

It took me a while to get past those blinders of being in a room in an office building and learning how to connect with listeners. Glenn was instrumental in getting me there.

As I got more comfortable with the audience, I got more comfortable talking about the issues I enjoy discussing. I love talking about the civil rights movement. I love talking about the Second Amendment. I love talking about the false perception that the Republican Party is filled with elites and not working-class, everyday people.

I like these conversations with listeners because I can be dispassionate but still get my point across. The abortion conversation is one I like to have as well, but it's a little harder with people because they believe what they believe. I would rather

Talking with Glenn Beck at his studio in Dallas, Texas.

talk about an issue and let my political view come out during the course of the discussion rather than just talk politics.

One example is when news broke about the mass shooting at Sandy Hook Elementary School. That day, I remember not wanting to go on the air. I was thinking, "How am I going to do this?" I was sitting in our newsroom and watching the death toll of these kids climb. Then we found out that this guy with a high-powered rifle murdered an entire classroom of first graders and his own mother.

I reached out to Glenn before my show. I said, "How am I going to do this? I can't ignore it. Everybody's talking about it. But how do I make sense of a kid who murders his mother at point-blank range and then murders a classroom full of first graders? How do you make any sense of that?"

Glenn told me to be honest about my feelings and be a voice of comfort, not division.

When the conversation turned to the Second Amendment, it became easier. You can't explain the demented mind of someone who is so devoid of reality that he would kill innocent children, but you certainly can't prevent those horrible acts by taking away law-abiding citizens' rights. When these things happen, it's always been my view that it's more about HIPAA (Health Insurance Portability and Accountability Act) laws than it is about gun laws.

I would love to talk to the most adamant anti–Second Amendment person and have him or her genuinely answer this question: How is disarming me or limiting my access to firearms making us safer? I will obey gun laws because I am a law-abiding citizen. A criminal won't. Criminals are going to break the law, conceal guns illegally, and use them in horrible situations. Without people like me around who are armed and willing to defend themselves and others, we're at the criminals' mercy. I just would love to have that conversation with someone.

During those three days I spent with Glenn in Dallas, I learned not only about top-tier broadcasting but also about his demanding schedule. I thought, "I'm never complaining about my schedule again." (Don't hold me to this.) The joke with everyone who has ever traveled anywhere with Glenn Beck is that no one sleeps. I don't know when he sleeps. He is always at 100 percent and maximizing every minute when he travels.

One of the lessons I've learned from Glenn that has made me better at my job is that I have to be transparent about who I am. Then, if somebody calls me names for it, I have to accept that that's how some people feel. No one knows that better than Glenn.

Glenn has made a career out of doing what he thinks is right. You have to admire and respect that regardless of whether you agree with him. He's a guy who made millions of dollars at Fox News and in radio. He could have lived a very comfortable life and been a rock star as the number-one guy on Fox News at the time. He could have continued there for another ten years, ended the Glenn Beck program on radio, and he would have been just fine. Instead he said, "I want to do something different," and he started TheBlaze. All the experts said to him, "Are you crazy? You're going to leave Fox News? You are going to become irrelevant. You are going to become nothing because you don't have that platform anymore." And he said, "I want to make a difference."

TheBlaze has grown into a phenomenal website. Then he launched TheBlaze news and entertainment network. It isn't about the money those things have generated. It's the fact that here's someone who says, "I don't want to do *just* this."

How many of us would aspire to have a show on Fox News? Or any of the lesser-watched cable networks? There are so many people who would give anything for that opportunity. Glenn, as I said, was the number-one guy on Fox News. It wasn't an arrogant move; he moved because he wanted to do more. He risked everything to do something he thought was right for him.

I admire that because he could have crashed and burned. Knowing Glenn as well as I do, he would have been okay crashing and burning doing what he wanted to do versus making a ton of money doing something that was no longer the right fit for him.

Having good mentors and people I admire in my life has been a great blessing. Ideally, you've got parents you admire. You may not always agree with them on everything, but you admire them and their work ethic. Lots of people, especially young women, admire Hillary Clinton. Despite jokes to the contrary, she's a human being like everybody else. If you rise and fall with the rise and fall of Hillary Clinton, then you have mentor issues. You should be admiring someone much closer to you. It should be a person who really has your best interests in mind. He or she should be someone who is invested in you specifically and talks about what's right and what's best for you. You never have to question this person's advice because he or she may have an agenda.

We have heroes in sports. What happens when we find out that one of those heroes is cheating by using steroids? What happens when we find out that one of those heroes breaks the law and goes to jail?

If you want to emulate somebody who is so removed from you that you've never met the person, then I feel bad for you. The person who should influence the way you behave and the way you think should be someone who knows you well enough to help you in the right way, and feels invested in your success as a person, not just in your career.

Mentors come through developing relationships. Don't go into any relationship thinking, "I want connections. I want a mentor." I wasn't looking for a mentor when I met Glenn. I merely expressed some exasperation with being new in the business I was in. He saw something in me and helped me. We developed a friendship. I have said to him on a number of occasions that he's the older brother I never had.

EVERYONE HAS A STORY THAT DESERVES TO BE HEARD

I'VE HAD THE PLEASURE of interviewing some pretty amazing guests: comedian and impersonator Frank Caliendo, Senator John McCain, rock-and-roll legends Ted Nugent and Alice Cooper, and Steve-O from the show *Jackass*, to name just a few.

They've all been great. You get to learn so much about people when they're open to talking about anything. Ted Nugent always has boundless energy. You're going to get Uncle Ted. He can go in a million directions, and every single one will be the right one.

Steve-O was one of my favorite interviewees because I didn't do the expected "tell me about your stunts, like when you jumped in the water and when you snorted wasabi" questions. Believe me, I wanted to ask because I love those *Jackass* movies. I don't know why they're so funny to me, but I cry watching them. Steve-O went to a college near where I grew up—the Ringling Brothers and Barnum & Bailey Clown College. It is where

Steve-O at the KFYI studio in Phoenix, Arizona.

people get trained to become circus clowns and other types of performers. The Ringling family built this college and donated a beautiful art museum in Sarasota, Florida. One of the things that Steve-O and I share is the loss of a loved one. Ryan Dunn, one of the *Jackass* stars and Steve-O's best friend, died in a car crash. The interview I did with Steve-O was more about who Ryan was as a person.

After we talked for a bit, I asked him, "I don't want to get too personal if you don't want to, but you've suffered a pretty big loss after your friend's death. How has that impacted you?"

It was a great interview. He was very pragmatic and thoughtful. There was a whole different side to him that people got to see in that interview, which was the guy sitting around the house with his friends and talking about stuff, as opposed to the guy just doing something stupid for the cameras or for the thrill of it.

When the interview was over, he said, "That was kind of cool. That was almost like therapy."

I could see it in his demeanor. He relaxed a little bit. He was willing to show a different, more personal side instead of the side that was Steve-O, the character.

Another one of my favorite interviews was with Alice Cooper on his foundation and the Solid Rock Teen Center in Phoenix that helps at-risk youths. He's gone from being a guy who parents didn't want kids to listen to because he was scary, to being a guy who does something amazing for kids in the community. Like me, he was able to stay out of trouble with drugs and other things in high school because of sports. He wanted to play baseball but ended up lettering in track and field. I had never pictured Alice Cooper in a letterman's jacket, which is one of the things that made the interview so interesting.

He said, "A teenager's worst enemy is too much time on his hands with nothing to do."

So, the Solid Rock Teen Center "cultivates a love of the arts to inspire and challenge teens to embrace artistic excellence and avoid drugs, guns, or gangs."

I'm enamored with people's stories a lot of times. There are a lot of people I will probably never get a chance to interview. I count myself lucky that I've already gotten to interview so many and share their stories with an audience. Whenever I talk with someone new, I think, "There's a story there, a life story that I could learn a lot from, and I'd love to be able to hear and share it." You don't need to have a radio or TV show to appreciate them, just listen to people.

Interviewing Alice Cooper for AZTV at his Solid Rock Foundation's Rock Teen Center.

The radio format doesn't always allow for really in-depth interviews, because it's in eight- and 10-minute snippets, but there's just a lot to be learned from people.

When you can drag out the stories people have never told, as in the case of Steve-O and his best friend's death from a car crash, the audience finds a new way to connect with them. Not everyone can relate to jumping off a bridge, but a lot of people can relate to loss.

I'm proof that everyone has a story to tell. Some of the best stories are just about the people you already know. Being able to talk is certainly an important part of talk radio, but listening, be it to someone you're interviewing or to the audience, is very important. I didn't write this book because I wanted to tell stories about me, but because I wanted to give credit and recognition to the people I've been lucky enough to know.

PAY ATTENTION TO
THE REAL HEROES AMONG US

MY BROTHER BRYAN WORKED HARD all throughout school. As I mentioned, he stayed focused and graduated from college with honors, and then followed his dream of joining law enforcement. He could've made a lot of money doing a lot of different things. He is honest to a fault and would've been an asset to any Fortune 500 company. Instead, he went into law enforcement, because when he was a kid, he lived in a safe place and wanted to make sure future generations had the same opportunity. He played Little League baseball and football in a safe little town. He wanted to keep it safe for his kids and other kids. This is the nobility of what he did and what he does every day.

I'm not blind to the danger he faces in his job, but I don't worry about my brother because he's so good at what he does. I do take it personally when I hear and see the disdain people have for law enforcement, because my brother is my hero. You'd better believe I'm going to have an opinion on multimillionaires who choose to kneel during the National Anthem because of perceived inequality and violence by police officers.

I know so many people in law enforcement, so I know Bryan and his wife, Jaime, who is also in law enforcement, are typical and not exceptions. They not only work their butts off to serve their community, but they also coach and mentor kids to try to develop an even better community. For them to be demonized and vilified for alleged racial profiling or being heavy-handed thugs is such a disservice, because the overwhelming majority of men and women who go into law enforcement do it as an act of service to their community. It's an act of humility, not arrogance. I can't stand the perception that it's for any other reason.

Bryan has taught me that doing the right thing the right way pays off. He's never going to be a household name, but he quietly contributes more to his community than I ever will to mine.

When I was in a bad place and Bryan was still in high school, I was saved by coming out of my own shell and trying to help somebody else. I decided I was going to improve myself for my brother's sake, and that's what saved me. If I hadn't decided that I needed to be there for my brother, and if I had never looked outside of myself to end my selfishness when I was young, I don't know where I would be. It was only because I wanted better things for Bryan that I actually became a better person.

Bryan has taught me selflessness. He has always done the right things for the right reasons. Bryan has never cheated or lied to anyone. He has never wrongfully arrested anyone. Although he's a huge man, he has never had a complaint against him for any type of abuse or misconduct. He has just been a solid, good police officer. He is also the best father I've ever seen. His three

Clockwise from left: Emily, me, Lauren, big Bryan, and Bryan Jr.

kids all play sports, and he never misses an event. Bryan and his wonderful wife live to make sure their kids get educated. Their older daughter rides horses and plays basketball. The younger daughter plays basketball and volleyball. Their youngest child, their son, plays basketball and soccer.

I don't claim any credit for Bryan's accomplishments. All I provided was an opportunity. People make choices to take advantage of opportunities or not. The opportunity I gave my brother was support. I just decided to be there. He had to choose what to do with his God-given talents.

My relationships with my brothers were solid. Bryan is genuinely my hero. There's not a person in the world I trust or connect with more. For that, I am eternally grateful. My brother carved a life for himself that is admirable and respectable. He is going to have a long-lasting effect, not only on the community he serves but also on the children he is raising. He and Jaime are just amazing with their kids. That in itself is an immeasurable, honorable thing, given the way we grew up.

You don't need to look to famous or fictional heroes for inspiration. There are plenty, like my brother Bryan, who are doing everything they can to ensure our safety and build a better community for future generations.

PRACTICE THE GIFT OF GIVING

ONE OF THE REASONS I was drawn to the trades is the satisfaction of being able to fix something. I saw my grandfather do it for the neighbors when they needed help with their cars or anything else. They usually paid him something, but he liked being the one people could count on when something was broken. For me, to be able to fix a machine or piece of equipment for a customer so he or she could get back to work, gave me a lot of gratification.

There's gratification not only in getting paid to do a job but also in being able to help somebody who is going through a tough time. As someone who benefited from others helping my mom and her kids, I know how important something as simple as a working car or a bag of groceries can be to a family.

I grew up with a St. Vincent de Paul's thrift store in my hometown, and there are many others across the U.S. In Phoenix, I got connected with the Society of St. Vincent de Paul as an adult when I realized it is an amazing organization. The largest commercial kitchen in Arizona is at St. Vincent de Paul. Over

3,000 meals every single day are served out of St. Vincent de Paul in dining halls across Arizona and in people's homes. It's just an amazing organization.

At the thrift store, staffers take donated items, resell them, and then use the money for the group's programs to help the poor. At Christmastime, one of the group's thrift stores in town has a day when elementary school kids can come in and buy any two items for a dollar each. If you can carry it out of the store, you can buy it for a dollar. Instead of these underprivileged kids getting free gifts for themselves, they get the opportunity to be the giver. There's nothing like that feeling of being able to give even when times are tough.

For a couple of years, I've done my show from the event and have met some of the kids and volunteers. At times, I was almost brought to tears by these kids' generosity and thoughtfulness. One of the items a kid bought was an oscillating fan. It was just a small tabletop fan. One of the volunteers from St. Vincent de Paul asked him, "Who's the fan for?"

He said, "It's for my mom. She's going through chemo and she's always hot, and I want her to be able to stay cool."

That kid was so proud to hand over his dollar and take home that gift for his mom.

Generally, people think of kids as being selfish and needing to be reined in. At a store, many kids want a toy and spend the trip asking, "Can I get this? Can I get this?" Kids are just naturally that way. To see the kids at this event think about their brothers or sisters or parents is so touching. To me it means more than anything else, because I found out later in life that the way for me out of poverty was through giving and learning a trade.

This Christmas shopping experience has now turned underprivileged kids who may be on the receiving end of assistance into givers. These kids have no idea that it's a charity event. They feel like they are really buying gifts for their loved ones. They really take the time to think about what their loved ones might need. Fostering that feeling of giving in young, underprivileged children is so powerful to me. It is one of my favorite events every year, and nobody does it better than St. Vincent de Paul.

If I see a man or woman with a ton of things in his or her car and I'm empty-handed, I'll ask if I can help carry something to the elevator. Giving isn't about making a grand gesture or just writing a check. It's as simple as saying to someone, "Your hands are full. Let me open the door for you."

It starts in your own sphere. It doesn't have to be at a charitable organization. You don't have to cure cancer. You don't have to do big things to make a difference. You can just find a small need that somebody has and fill it.

Giving is also about investing your time in people. It is one thing to hand a homeless person a dollar. That's very helpful. It's a completely different thing to have a conversation with homeless people about who they are and treat them like normal human beings. One of my heroes growing up was my cousin Kenny. He was a year older than me. Kenny had a serious drug and alcohol problem, and ended up homeless on the streets of Las Vegas. When I last saw him, he was still the hero I looked up to as a kid, but he was homeless and he looked it. He had the long, shaggy hair, the mismatched clothes, and was dirty. But when I saw him it felt like going back in time and hanging out. I'd walk around Vegas with him and we would just talk.

He ended up having seizures caused from so many years of drug abuse and died in the desert of Las Vegas at a homeless camp.

Like Kenny, every one of those people on the streets has a story. Many of them are there by their own doing. They would admit that. Their addictions and other issues got them there. But they're still human beings. To not just hand somebody a dollar out of your car window, but to walk into a convenience store with a homeless person and talk with him or her like they're a normal person and not some kind of an outcast, is important.

One Thanksgiving, there were a couple of homeless guys that hung around the convenience store by my house. My family had Thanksgiving dinner, and there were five or six kids at the house. We loaded up paper plates of food and dessert, along with plastic forks, knives, and napkins. I took all the kids with me to visit with these two homeless guys at the convenience store, and we just gave them dinner. Then we stood around and we talked to them for a little while. I wanted those kids to see them as people and to see that everybody has a story, and everybody has choices.

Giving starts in your own home and neighborhood. Soften your heart to your brothers and sisters or to your parents or to whoever else is in your home. Help the elderly woman across the street dragging her garbage can down to the end of the street or driveway. If you see somebody on the side of the road who is dressed up in nice clothes with a flat tire, change the tire for him or her. No excuses—if you've read this book, that's a skill you have now!

USE YOUR INSECURITIES
AS MOTIVATORS

THERE ARE TWO THINGS that get under my skin, and they aren't the things you would think would bother me. (No, it's not my hair!) One is questioning my intelligence, and the other is questioning my motives.

When something gets under your skin, it's because you think maybe there's a hint of truth to it. If somebody calls me an elitist, I laugh my head off. In a way it's a compliment, because the person obviously has no idea where I've come from. If I present myself now as some kind of an elitist with a silver-spoon upbringing, man, have I come a long way from my white trash roots!

People are not shy about saying horrible things to me. There was a general contractor in Phoenix who sent an e-mail that said, "Shut up about being a contractor. You suck. Stop talking about your dead brother. He chose to go in the military and knew the risks."

I thought it was funny that this guy had chosen to denigrate and mock me about my brother. This random guy who had nothing better to do but e-mail a stranger is just showing himself as a fool. Those kinds of e-mails never get under my skin, because I know they're just uninformed. However, when somebody starts talking about my lack of intelligence or lack of preparedness for my show, it instantly gets under my skin. I know that comes from the fact that I'm not college-educated. I live and work in a world where education is key. I can keep up with the news and read everything, but that's not going to give me the college degree that some people use to judge intelligence.

I am self-educated. Despite barely having a high school diploma, I wanted to challenge myself by taking a college course, because I do have that sore spot about education. When I took Political Ideology and Worldview at Arizona Christian University, I hadn't been in a classroom as a student in twenty-five years. I have the intellect for school, but I never had the discipline.

I actually knew the president of the university and the professor of the class. My first thought was that these people are now going to know what an idiot I really am. I was going to have to write papers. The professor was going to read them and realize that all of this stuff I was spewing on the air was not coming from an educated position. As it turned out, I ended up flourishing in this class. It was easy in the sense that I loved the work, and the process of thinking critically about issues presented in the class made sense to me.

Over the course of the semester, conveying a thought on paper became much easier, and I aced the class. I was very proud of myself, because I knew I earned everything that made up that A. I wish I could say I've gotten my political science degree, but I haven't.

Education has become more important to me as I've gotten older, but when someone questions my intellect, that gets under my skin because there's a hint of truth to it. I don't like that I have the sore spot, but I use my lack of a formal education to motivate me to become more proficient in the issues that are important to me and important to know in today's political climate.

The other thing that gets under my skin, as I said, is when someone questions my motives. On the radio I work very, very hard to show both sides of an argument. Even if I disagree with someone, I'll give that person a platform. I'll let him either make a point that's valid or give him enough rope to hang himself. That's only fair. I don't skate over one person and rake somebody else over the coals. I don't do hit-piece journalism. So, when people accuse me of that, it's a snapshot of who I am in their mind. That assumption is enough to get a reaction from me, because I know in my heart that I work to give my listeners an honest shot at hearing all sides of an issue, so I feel the need to defend myself.

Recently, I was talking about North Korea and Donald Trump. I had a guy on my show from Virginia who does talk radio in Richmond. We posted the conversation on Facebook, and a guy posted about what a jerk I am. He said I pretend to have blue-collar roots, but now I hang out with the elites in Arizona. I didn't even get mad at the guy. I wrote to him, "You need to rethink how you do things." I love God, and I love my family, and I love my country. I try to serve all of them as best as I can, and I'm not perfect. I wrote, "I assure you my intentions are as genuine or as pure as yours are."

I don't hold that guy's opinion against him. I know where I come from and how lucky I am to be where I am now. I'm the luckiest guy in the entire world. I have a great life, and I love what I do. I don't need the affirmation of people who don't know me. The people who love me, love me. As for the people who don't know me or do know me and still don't like me—well, they're entitled to their opinions, too.

I learned from my grandfather that I'm never going to please everybody. Sure, I want to try and I want to be liked, but at the end of the day, I have to look in the mirror and know who I am. I'm not ashamed of where I've come from. I am ashamed of the mistakes I've made and the things I wish I had done differently. Rather than dwell on them, I use those experiences to motivate me to do better.

YOUR COURSE IS NOT DETERMINED BY ANYONE BUT GOD

IF YOU'VE LEARNED ANYTHING from this book and my random collection of stories, it's that no one's course is destined to be a certain way just because he or she is born to certain circumstances. People's lives can be changed by the people who invest in them and by investing in others.

I had to walk a really dark path when my brother was killed. Faith has played an extremely important role in my life. You'll never convince me that God does not exist.

I was the family spokesman. As an officiant at my brother's funeral, I worked with the Army chaplain to organize the services and logistics, because I wanted to make things easier for my family. There were times when I had to get up to speak, especially in the beginning, when I was praying and talking to God to be able to get through it. I would just say to myself while I was waiting to speak, "I have no idea what to say to these people.

God, you're going to have to do it for me, because I don't have any idea what I am going to say."

I would get up and I would speak. When I was done, people would come up, hug me, and tell me how much it meant to them. I would never get a swelled head over anything they said, because I honestly don't remember much of what I said despite speaking three times at my brother's funeral.

No one will convince me that God didn't have His hand on my shoulder walking through those times. I was certainly not strong enough to go through them on my own. I don't care about denominational differences, because my foundation is in faith and God's role in my life. I don't care if you're Lutheran, Catholic, or Baptist. I know He exists, and therefore all the other stuff is more how we practice as opposed to the accuracy of it.

After I did that first guest shot on the radio station, when the station manager said to me, "Man, you're good at this. Do you want a job?" I could have said, "No, I'm not. I'm not good at it at all," then continued doing what I was doing.

But I feel like I'm where I'm supposed to be in my current job in broadcasting and public speaking. It has given me freedom and the opportunity to make a difference in a way that I never expected. I firmly believe that I didn't put myself here. God did. There's no way I could have created this career for myself. Anybody who has ever been in the media knows that what has happened to me does not happen to people looking for a broadcasting career. That's why I take my job and my faith very seriously.

God maneuvered this career for me in an unexpectedly rapid way. When it's over and it's time for me to do something else, regardless of whether I am firing on all cylinders and hitting ratings out of the park, it's going to be over. There's freedom in knowing it's in God's hands. I work hard and I do my best, but I'm not driving the ship. I love that feeling. That's why I'm so comfortable in my job, and that's why I love what I do. For the first time in my life, I feel like I'm exactly where I'm supposed to be in my career.

It's easy to be frustrated with God's timeline for your life. But once you let go of the expectations you have for yourself, God will bless you with more than you ever thought possible.

ONCE YOU THINK YOU'RE HUMBLE, YOU'RE NOT

ONE OF MY BEST MENTORS on my faith journey is my friend and pastor Robb Williams. When we first met up for coffee after church, I knew we'd get along, because as we sat outside the coffee shop, we made fun of the same people walking by us. We just cracked each other up. Robb has often told jokes about humility. He said, "You know, the funny thing about humility is, the minute you think you have it, you don't. The minute you say, 'Man, am I humble,' you're not that at all."

Anybody who knows me knows there's an edge to me that I don't always like. It comes out when someone tells me I can't do something.

I have always joked around, and I know this joke's been told a thousand times, but I've said to people, "You know, there's a really good chance that my last words are going to be, 'Watch this.'" There were a couple of times when it could have been.

Don't tell me it's impossible, because the egomaniac in me says, "Yes, I can. Yes, I will."

I'm fifty-one years old, but my head and heart don't know it. Just a few months ago I injured my shoulder in the gym, because no one was going to tell me, "No, you can't. That's too much weight."

Humility doesn't come from being a humble person. For me, humility comes from my faith and the realization that I have gone through times when I knew in my heart that I wasn't going to get through it. In my heart, I didn't know how I was going to endure it. When I did get on the other side of it, not only had I endured it, but I was able to help people. I can guarantee you that didn't come from me, because I'm an egomaniac like anybody else, and I was humbled by God.

That's the dichotomy of faith and humility when it comes to listening to other people's advice. There are two ways that you have to handle those situations in your life. One is to listen, because somebody may make a valid point. The other is to decide whether it's advice you can use to improve your life.

Your grandfather could say to you, "You need to go to college, and you need to get a biology degree in order to be successful."

You may decide to do it and go get a degree. Then someone says to you, "Why did you get a degree in biology?"

You say, "Well, my grandfather was a biology major, and he told me I needed to get a degree, so I did it because he did it."

The person then says, "Well, do you want to be a biologist?"
You say, "No, I hate it."

"So, then what are you going to do with the rest of your life?"

"Get a college education" is a valid piece of advice for a lot of people. But before making the decision based on ego and thinking, "Everyone else has one, and what does it say about me if I don't?" Instead, humble yourself and think about why you really want it.

One misconception about me, as well as about a lot of others in the media, is that nothing bothers me. People think the things around me do not affect me, and that I have a thick shell because of my job or life experiences. But just like everyone else, I can be lonely or self-conscious, doubt my abilities, and sometimes have to deal with other self-esteem issues.

I think a lot of misconceptions come from people seeing just a snapshot of someone they don't know. The same thing happens when someone gives you advice—that person has only a snapshot of your situation. If you regularly listen to my show, you probably listen only fifteen to thirty minutes a day, or maybe a little more if your commute is longer. Even then, I am as real as I can be on the air, but it's not the totality of who I am. I think people have snapshots of who I am, but there are not many people who really, really know me. Writing this book was like going through therapy. While some aspects of my life are unique, I know a lot of people can also relate to the same struggles I've had.

Being open to criticism or observations about yourself and your actions is valuable. We all have self-esteem issues. We all think weird things about ourselves. It's saying them out loud or hearing about them from others that can be difficult. You've got to reconcile those things in yourself.

What I mean by that is, let's say you believe something about yourself and you hate it. Instead of thinking, "Well, you know what? That's not necessarily true" and then somebody confirms it for you and you're like, "Damn it! I guess it is true," reconcile that within your mind and move on. In the grand scheme of things, it's okay because we all have those things we wish we could change about ourselves. Faith reminds us there are bigger issues.

For example, I joke about getting older and I joke about getting hair transplants or whatever would work, because I'd do it in a minute if it looked good. I'm talking about my 1980s glory-days hair, not Joe Biden hair plugs. I know I'm losing my hair. It's apparent. I'm not fooling anybody with my U hat, nor am I trying. One day, my TV producer said to me, "Man, it looks like you're losing more hair."

I said, "You're getting more wrinkles."

She said, "I know. Screw you." We laughed about it, because nobody wants to hear it but it's reality. There's freedom in just accepting it. God is my barber, so what can I do?

TRUST EMPLOYEES AND MAKE THEM PART OF THE VISION

FROM MY EXPERIENCE IN MANAGEMENT and owning my own company, the best way to motivate employees is to let them do their jobs the way they want to within the parameters of what you need. In construction, I say to somebody, "I need to get this job done as quickly as possible," because I'm paying people by the hour. I don't want to waste money on material and labor if the job can be done more quickly and with the same quality. I also don't want to go to a jobsite with a worker who looks at me and thinks, "Uh-oh, the boss is here."

That's not how I want employees to feel. I want them to feel like they've been hired to do the job because I trust that they can do the job. Then I let them do their job. If the job is finished in the time frame you need and under budget, then reward them. Thank and reward them. If there's a financial reward, that's great, but let them know you appreciate their work. People don't feel invested in a job if they feel like their work is overlooked.

The best way to motivate employees is not by reminding them that you're the boss and they're the employees; it's by showing them you're partners in a job that needs to get done. They've agreed to a certain amount of money, and you've agreed to pay them that amount of money for the job they're doing.

If they do the job and you write them the check, that's a partnership. You want them to know that you have a vision of where you want to go with the company. Tell them and show them that you would like for them to be a part of it. They are not just tools in that vision, but they are in on a partnership to make it happen so everyone can be successful. As an employee, you would put in extra work for this type of company. In a partnership, it works both ways.

I've worked with all generations. I certainly see the world differently at fifty-one, but the one constant is that people want to be part of a winning team. I have an eighteen-year-old intern. I have a tech director and a board operator in their early twenties. My news director and producer are also at least ten years younger than me. They all have a different view of the world than I do at fifty-one. I also have great sponsors who have supported the show. The motivation to be successful is still the same for all of us.

You might think the tech director's job is to just push the buttons and make sure we're on the air. Well, I want that guy to feel like he's a part of the team, because he is. Everybody's replaceable, including me. I could be replaced tomorrow, and within twenty-four hours, every reference to me could be wiped off the radio station. Six months later, nobody would remember my name. That's a fact. I want everybody to feel like we're doing this together. People rally around the idea of being a part of a team that's accomplishing something bigger than just showing up to a job pushing buttons.

I'm the host of *The Mike Broomhead Show*, but without my team, I'm just a guy talking to himself in a room. And without the sponsors, I'm just a guy talking to himself on a street corner. Everyone there is the best in the business, and I'm glad we're all a team. They make me look better than I actually am.

WE ALL HAVE THREE THINGS
TO OFFER THE WORLD

MONEY, TALENT, AND TIME. WE all have these things to varying degrees. There are times in my life when I've had no money but tons of time.

When I was an electrician, I would volunteer with church groups to go to the Navajo Nation here in Arizona, and we'd work on building and remodeling their churches. I had that talent, so I could fix lights and replace things. I was able to offer talent and time, but I didn't necessarily have money. Now I'm older and I make a nice living in radio and television. So I've got money, but I don't have a lot of time. When possible, I can offer my talent as an emcee or a speaker at an event, especially when it's for a cause that's important to me, and my participation can help raise more money and awareness for the cause.

Time becomes more valuable as I get older. I wish I were better at time management and not so scattered. I keep my schedule in my phone, and sometimes people ask if I'm available at some time months from now. I laugh at myself, and I look at my phone and I think, "Who in the world has things scheduled four months from now?" You know who does? People who are better at time management than I am.

As busy as I think I am now, I also know that I have a lot more freedom than people like Sean Hannity and Glenn Beck, who are truly at the top of their field. I've got a successful show and everything's going well. However, when I traveled with Glenn, I saw what it was like a couple of levels above me. We flew on a private jet to DC for events he had to do. When you're with people like him, you're traveling in blacked-out SUVs and you're running from one place to the next. It never feels like power and fame. You never feel like you're an elitist with him. It's not like you're being chauffeured from one place to another. You're basically being herded like cattle.

In between events, Glenn and I were talking about life, and he said to me, "I'm jealous of you." I know he was being honest, but I didn't know what the hell he was talking about. I said, "How in the world could you be jealous of me?"

He said I was lucky to have contact with listeners. He said there are times when it is easy to feel removed from his listeners. He told me to not ever lose contact with listeners, the real people.

I've really taken that to heart. I would love to have a national radio show, just like anybody in my business would. I would love for it to be of the caliber of Rush Limbaugh, Sean Hannity, or Glenn Beck. But I will never sacrifice that for the relationship I have with the people in my community.

For example, I was at a Fry's grocery store. I was at the self-service checkout, and one of the employees yelled, "Mike!" I looked over and I had no idea who this person was, but he looked at me like he knew me. He said, "You're Broomhead?"

"Yeah," I said. He walked over and said, "My wife and I listen to your show every day. I knew that was you. I knew it was you."

I thought, "How cool is it that this guy feels comfortable to come up to me?" It was like we were already friends despite the fact that I had never met him before in my life.

I never want to lose that ability to connect with the people I'm talking with every day. I pour my heart out to them every day about what I think, whether they agree or disagree, I never want to lose that connection. I never want to lose the ability to feel like they can walk up to me anytime and we can have a conversation.

When Glenn said he was jealous, I thought he was crazy until he explained himself. As I thought about it, I realized he was right. I'd love to have his life. I'd love to have his influence. I'd love to have his money. But, man, I do have something that he doesn't. I still have contact with my community, and he put it into perspective for me. In that moment, I felt really proud of what I had with listeners and the people in my community. I want people to know that if they reach out to me on social media, I'm the one who is going to respond. That goes for the haters, too—they're talking to a real person.

The three things you have to offer—money, talent, and time—may vary in quantity throughout your life. It's important to use them in ways that improve your life, your family, and your community.

YOU CAN CHANGE YOUR MIND
WITHOUT CHANGING YOUR PRINCIPLES

WE ALL DISAGREE ABOUT ISSUES. We all change our minds about issues. Often, changing your mind can be a good thing. It may lead to new opportunities, and professional or personal growth. In political terms, when politicians change their minds about something and we disagree, we call them flip-floppers. When they change to a position we agree with, we say they've evolved.

One example I've used, as unfortunate as it is for people, is marriage and divorce. There's a big shift in mindset when it comes to those issues. You know you were doing the right thing when you said, "I do." You know you were doing the right thing when you said, "I don't." In life we have to be flexible enough to admit: "That was my belief for noble reasons. My ideology hasn't changed. My principles haven't changed, but my perspective has. What I believed then was the right thing, but it might not be the right thing now."

You can stick to your principles and still be flexible in changing your mind about an issue. A political example is that I supported the Patriot Act. The Patriot Act was introduced after 9/11, and it included the surveillance of inbound phone calls from known terrorist countries, and searches previously prohibited by the Fourth Amendment. In my mind, it was an important tool in stopping the next 9/11, so, like a lot of people, I supported the Patriot Act.

People from all over the political spectrum, but especially libertarians, criticized the Patriot Act based on the slippery-slope argument and it opening the door to government surveillance that would go beyond the war on terrorism.

Then, we saw the National Security Agency, the facilities it was building, and the government surveillance of citizens. After I learned more about how the government was using the Patriot Act as cover to do a lot of things Americans didn't think it would do, I wasn't afraid to admit that I was 100 percent wrong. The Patriot Act was a noble idea to the people who supported it, but it became dangerous down the road.

The older I get, the more libertarian I become in my social views. I've always believed that the government has no business in the the institution of marriage. Marriage is a rite, not a right. It's a religious ceremony.

If you're someone who believes in God, it's a promise you make involving you, your partner, and God. If you are a same-sex couple and you can find a church that performs that rite, go for it. If you are a religious leader and your congregation believes you are going against God's will by marrying a same-sex couple, make your case or find another congregation. There is a theological argument on the issue of gay marriage, so that's something churches will have to decide among themselves.

Unfortunately, our government has inserted itself into the institution of marriage. Think about it: what is the purpose of the government issuing a license? I was a business owner. I got a business license. I got a driver's license at sixteen. If I get parking or speeding tickets, and don't pay them or cause a bunch of accidents, the government will take away my driver's license. If a restaurant owner serves alcohol to minors, the government can revoke the restaurant's liquor license.

The government issues a marriage license. Have you ever heard of a marriage license being revoked? Has a government agent ever said to a married couple, "The police have been to your house for domestic violence issues five times. You guys suck at this. We're revoking your marriage license"? Has the government ever refused to give a marriage license based on past behavior? Imagine a clerk saying, "You know what? You've been married four times in your life. We're not giving you a fifth marriage license. You suck at marriage."

I'm being slightly sarcastic, but the government's involvement in licensing marriages is silly and unnecessary. I have my personal beliefs about relationships, but the government has no business in that. If the government is going to give a license to one couple, it has to give it to all couples. The government boxed itself into a corner on the gay-marriage issue.

On marijuana legalization, I had friends while growing up who smoked all the time. Some lives were affected by it and some weren't. I can honestly say that I've never done it. I just never wanted to smoke pot. I don't have a desire to inhale anything into my lungs. There's nothing about it that's attractive to me.

I see both sides to the issue as being equally strong, and I can be pulled in either direction. I feel like a hypocrite because I can't pick a side sometimes. If America decides it wants to legalize marijuana, what do I care if it doesn't affect me? If Americans realize they don't want to have one more vice legalized, and they want to leave it illegal, I'm okay with that, too. I find myself being pulled in both directions.

Many people are saying, "Which is better, for it to be legalized or not legalized?" No one wants to say, "Well, I don't know." Everybody wants to be on the right side or have the right answer. But there's freedom and maturity in just admitting, "You know what? I don't know. I don't have all the answers."

I have the privilege of speaking to high school students a lot here in Arizona. It is one of my favorite things in the world to do, because high school kids talk about the same things that adults do. They just talk about them differently. They're scared about terrorism. They care about jobs being available. Rather than lecture, I let them ask questions and do my best to answer them.

When hard questions come up about abortion in the case of rape, or legalization of marijuana, I think kids respect that sometimes I have to say, "Listen, I don't know. You are catching me on questions I can't answer." Being able to be honest with a bunch of kids and say, "I don't have an answer" as a fifty-year-old guy is a good lesson for them. As adults, we don't have all the answers. A lot of times we end up having more questions. There's more freedom in talking with kids because they respect me for saying, "I don't know." In my experience, it's adults who are more likely to get frustrated by the answer "I don't know." Often, they aren't looking for answers, but for confirmation of what they already believe.

I am a registered Republican because I'm someone who believes the party's principles still matter. I hope that the party can get back on track and do the right thing by the country. I'm not leaving. I'm not becoming an Independent. But there are times when I look at my friends who are Independent and I think, "You know what? I don't blame you."

Ultimately, I think there is a set of principles that the Republican Party is supposed to advocate. Do I really want to fight this mess and wear that label, or should I just check out and be an Independent? I would rather stay inside and tell my Libertarian and Independent friends to come back and help me fix this place.

But maybe tomorrow, I'll change my mind.

PAY ATTENTION TO PEOPLE, NOT POLITICS

AS I'VE EXPRESSED EARLIER, my relationship with my father was very strained. Fortunately, we were able to bury the hatchet before he died. It was a friendly relationship, but it was never a father-and-son relationship. A piece of me has kind of longed for one. I didn't realize the depth of that type of relationship until I spent time with Senator John McCain.

It's funny, because I am as headstrong and stubborn as John McCain is. I have very strong beliefs. There is no one else who knows more about foreign policy than John McCain. Of course, I find myself disagreeing with him on some issues. Here's that arrogance I wrote about earlier when I said I don't always come from a place of humility. I'm an egomaniac. I will say things as if I'm an authority and I know what I'm talking about, but like anyone else, that's not always the case. He talks to me like I'm a peer, which is surreal, to be honest. He defends his position and has the conversation without belittling anyone. He's always been so good to me. I've been to his offices in DC and Phoenix. He would have his shoes off and his feet on the coffee table, telling me stories, laughing, and treating me like a colleague.

I admire him because he's talked about his time in the POW camp at the Hanoi Hilton. This was a guy who was so physically injured, he never fully recovered. To hear him talk about his time there—saying that those soldiers were some of the best friends he ever made and those were some of the best memories he has because of the patriotism he witnessed—just leaves me in awe. John McCain is a hero, regardless of how you feel about him politically.

Here's a guy whose father was an admiral. The Viet Cong were going to let him go as part of a propaganda message to tell the world, "See, we treat our prisoners well. We let Admiral McCain's son go," and John McCain refused to leave. They beat him and injured him so severely that he never had the same use of his arms ever again in his life. That is an American hero. Politically, there are times when I shake my head and say, "What the hell are you doing, Senator?" But I will always separate those disagreements from the person I know.

I was about to go on air when everyone found out he had been diagnosed with brain cancer. I prepared: diagnosis, this is where he's at, here is what's happening, the Mayo Clinic, all the basic facts. I wanted to be the most informed guy in the country, because he was my senator and getting treatment in my state.

Then I went on the air and for the first hour, I was mostly tongue-tied and dumbfounded. It hit me personally. I thought, "Man, I love that old man." I hadn't realized it and I thought about how good he'd been to me personally, not politically. I did not think about my disagreements with him. I just loved him.

After he was diagnosed, had his surgery, went back to DC and made those controversial votes on the healthcare bill, and returned to Phoenix to begin treatments. I landed the first interview he gave in the entire country about these experiences. It took place in my studio. He said to my audience and to everybody else, "You've agreed with me; you've disagreed with me. That's your job. You've always been fair."

He hugged me when he came into the studio. I don't expect the people who see just American politics to get it. But for me, John McCain is not just a senator from Arizona. He's John McCain, the man who had been diagnosed with a terrible disease, and a friend. There must have been a lot of self-reflection and the need to make sure he did things the right way. One of those things was to come on my local show first. That's huge in my heart.

That's about the man John McCain, not Senator John McCain, not Navy Pilot John McCain, not POW John McCain. That's the eighty-plus years of life experience, "I do what I want to do" John McCain, and I will never forget that as long as I live.

I've had private conversations with him with no microphones, in which he had a distant look in his eye and a smile on his face about being a POW, but he told stories of amazing patriotism, character, and camaraderie. Nobody wants to be a POW. But what he has carried through his whole career has been finding joy and contentment in doing the right thing, even in the worst of circumstances.

Whether it's getting his ass kicked and his bones broken because he wouldn't, as a POW, leave when given the chance, or getting ripped by the Republican Party and President Trump because he voted no on the "skinny repeal" healthcare bill, he

Senator John McCain in the KFYI studio.

doesn't strike me as a guy who's going to blink when that criticism comes. He doesn't care as long as he knows he's doing the right thing for the right reasons. I learned that from him.

The best moments I've shared with Senator McCain were when he was just talking about his time as a POW. One of the best is when he talked about a code he and the other POWs would tap on the walls to each other. He tapped on the desk where we were sitting and showed me how they would communicate. I said, "Wait a minute. Wait a minute. We've got to talk about this on the air."

We scrapped everything planned for the interview about foreign policy, taxes, and everything else, and I just asked him about those stories.

Basically, he and the other POWs broke the alphabet into three segments. The first tap was whether the letter was in segment one, two, or three. Then, it was which letter it was in the alphabet from there. Instead of the word "and," they would just hit the letter "N" to abbreviate it. I said to Senator McCain, "You guys were text messaging on the walls of the Hanoi Hilton."

He laughed about it. "Yeah, I guess we were. We were abbreviating."

To hear him tell those stories of how someone communicated four cells over with somebody else because the people in between passed it along was just remarkable. He shared his experiences that you might only read in history textbooks. He's a guy who actually lived it and is telling these stories.

It's those moments that kept them going in prison. He said that the enemy tried to isolate a person. If they could isolate you, then they could break you down. But the POWs would communicate and not be isolated from one another.

The Viet Cong were constantly trying to get POWs to disavow America. Every morning, one POW named Mike Christian would hang his shirt on the wall and everybody would stand and say the Pledge of Allegiance to the American flag sewn on his shirt. It was one of the most consequential moments of their day. He made a needle out of bamboo and collected random red and white fabrics he found. The clothing they were given was blue, so that was covered. He got caught and they stripped him down. They beat him mercilessly. When they finally dragged him back to be with the general population in the prison, the first thing he did was sew another American flag inside of his shirt. His face was beaten swollen and bloody, but he sat there sewing the American flag with a bamboo needle. He wasn't doing it for himself, but for his fellow soldiers so they could say the Pledge of Allegiance together.

When you go to a sporting event and they play the National Anthem, imagine its significance for John McCain and those who have served and are serving. Think of people like Mike Christian and remember what he did to honor his country and flag. Then think about the outrage when someone burns that flag on a sidewalk at a protest. Think of the football players who kneel and claim some sort of moral superiority because of it. There are lots of ways to protest and speak up about injustice. People would be more receptive to listening to them if they didn't tie their cause to the flag that men and women have literally bled and died to protect.

Everyone has an opinion about every politician and public figure. I've learned that my job is to give my opinion, and with that comes the hate mail. I get that people don't like me and don't like some of the people I call friends, people like John McCain and Glenn Beck. One thing I admire about Glenn is that he's a guy who is very transparent about the way he lived his life before he became the person we see today. It's almost like he has forgiven himself but has not forgotten, in a good way, those things about himself in the past.

Glenn is as busy a person as I've ever met, but when I'm with him, he makes me feel like I'm the only person in the world who matters. For him to be the older brother figure I never had is hysterical, because he and John McCain are polar opposites. There is an animosity that has never been reconciled between them and with some on the right, but I love them both.

Glenn has genuinely been the older brother I never had. He has reached out when I've had horrible things going on in my life, just to check on me and see how I'm doing. I'm always touched when he's juggling ten balls in the air at the same time, and yet finds time to reach out to me. Anti-Trump, Never Trump... whatever it is, I don't care. We disagree, but that doesn't change my opinion of him personally.

Glenn isn't somebody who squashes somebody else's opinion. He could get a number of radio hosts to fill in for him who would just parrot all of his opinions. Instead, he calls me. Glenn is somebody who wants somebody on the air who's going to be honest. I'll go on the air for him and I may disagree with a lot of points he's made, but he just wants me to be honest about what I believe.

The "people over politics" attitude I take is best showcased in the nonfamily family I've cultivated over the years. Glenn Beck is like my big brother, and John McCain is like my father. Now that would be a rowdy Thanksgiving dinner.

REALITY COMES FROM EXPERIENCE IN THE REAL WORLD

IF I LISTENED ONLY to the media after my brother's death in Iraq, I might think that Cindy Sheehan's view was how all Americans felt. Fortunately, the vast majority of people I know and got to know through that experience were supportive, loving, and kind. So when I saw the media's portrayal of the war and America's response, it was easy to see it was outside the norm. The media was on the anti-war side (at least until 2008) and made it a priority to give the anti-war people a platform. It was laughable, because their cameras were focused on 200 people jumping up and down and screaming about President Bush having blood on his hands, but what I saw were 300 people in a small town at a dedication and a memorial for one person—my brother.

My concern is that many people have chosen to isolate themselves from their community and media with whom they disagree. Many are reading what they want to read as opposed to paying attention to the reality around them. One example is the media's newfound obsession with the white supremacist "move-ment." Reality comes from experience, and experience tells me in my life that white supremacy is dwindling, not rising. It's looked upon like it was in the 1970s, when I saw it as archaic and found white supremacists to be borderline mentally deranged. They are a small group of people who are just so angry that they couldn't see beyond blaming others for their problems. So, when you see the news segments and articles, which state white supremacy is on the rise, and if that idea doesn't sit well with what you see in your everyday life, then trust your own experience.

I may be immersed in conservative radio, but I live in the real world. Nobody I know defends or sympathizes with white supremacists. Not one. I've also never come into contact with any white supremacists. As a matter of fact, if one thing would motivate conservatives to action, it would be to shout down the Klan or the neo-Nazis. No one wants to be associated with them. They are among the most reprehensible, yet the media is happy to give them a platform.

Here's another example that's less serious. There are people out there who dedicate their lives to finding Bigfoot. When they talk amongst themselves, there is no doubt that Bigfoot exists. I watch *Finding Bigfoot* on Animal Planet religiously every week, because it is the funniest show on television. It stars four grown adults, and three of them are convinced of the existence of Bigfoot. Every week, they are in a different place. Every week, they come so close to getting proof but just miss it. And I couldn't care less. So I look at that and I think, "If you're someone who is so dedicated to that, good for you." But there's not a single person in my everyday life who says, "I care whether Bigfoot exists or not."

If you're wrapped up in worrying about the white supremacist movement, you should know that nobody cares except the members of the media, and that's because they have their own agenda. Likewise, Animal Planet doesn't care whether Bigfoot exists, just that people want to watch the show. The vast majority of people do not think about white supremacy until it's in the news.

To those who aren't sure about whether this so-called movement exists, I'd say look around you. Have you seen a rise in white supremacy in your town since the election of Donald Trump? Have you seen it in your family? Does it seem like there are more people looking at the idea of white supremacy or Nazism, and it's something they consider a good thing?

Take a look at who the president has appointed to his cabinet: Steven Mnuchin, who is Jewish; Ben Carson, who is African-American; Nikki Haley, who is an Indian-American; Elaine Chao, who is an Asian-American. You can look at the fact that Donald Trump is the first sitting American president to pray at the Western Wall in Israel. There is enough evidence to say whether you like him, or you don't like him. You may hate his policies. You may hate his tweets. You may never vote for him in a million years. There is enough anecdotal evidence to show you that he can be completely wrong on a bunch of things. That doesn't make him a neo-Nazi or a white supremacist.

If you're selling shoes, you are going to tell somebody, "These are the greatest shoes that have ever been made. These are the most amazing shoes, and with these shoes you can run faster, and you can walk longer, and your back's never going to hurt. These are going to last a lifetime."

The average person knows it's just a pair of shoes. So ask yourself, "What is the media selling me?" If you're CNN or any of the other news agencies, what sells right now is fear, bashing Donald Trump and calling him a white supremacist. It's based on an ideological agenda, a ratings agenda, or both. You've always got to consider the motivation of the people who are selling you a narrative.

GOD HAS A PLAN, AND SOMETIMES IT SUCKS

DURING TIMES OF STRIFE, we often say and hear that God has a plan. Sometimes it seems like an empty statement that's made because people don't know what else to say when tragedy happens. They just say, "God has a plan."

I've put my life in God's hands, but there have been times when I admit, "Man, I hate this plan so far. I have no idea what it is, but this plan sucks right now." It's hard to have patience, because you don't know why some things happen, but I honestly believe there are things we can't understand yet. It gives me enough to get through the day. It's very difficult, because I would trade every minute of this career, every single minute of it, for just ten more minutes with my brother without batting an eye. That's not possible, so instead I must go along with whatever God has in store for me.

I can't change what has happened in my life, and you can't change what has happened in your life. There are no refunds. But what we can do is realize that if we're mindful and faithful, we can still be used in a way that ends up with a positive outcome. Our pain can have a purpose. I understand those who are so angry that they don't see the positive yet, or think it's too early or not possible to carry on beyond grief. I would tell them that grief can be used to help other people in a way you never imagined if you just move forward.

I used to joke that I never wanted grandkids to call me Grandpa or Granddad. Instead I wanted to be called Coach. I didn't see myself as old enough to be a "grand" anything. Now I know that some of the greatest gifts come before you think you're ready, or they come in a different way than you may have imagined.

Likewise, I felt like Forrest Gump years ago when I had the honor of being with Gold Star Families United and speaking on the National Mall. Looking out and seeing the Washington Monument, the Lincoln Memorial, and all those people out on the National Mall waiting for us to speak brought me to tears. As an American, I found it moving just to be there. I remember sitting there completely by myself, crying and thinking, "My gosh, what am I doing here?"

My perspective on life changed later in life when I was an adult. I started to see people in the Bible not as abstract but as actual people. And whether or not you're a Christian, whether or not you believe that the Bible was inspired, whether or not you believe that Jesus is really the son of God, the people written about in the Bible are real. The Bible is pretty well documented as a history book, so we know those people existed. When I started to think of people in the Bible as human beings who faced the same kind of pressures, and challenges, and defeat that I have, I better understood that only faith matters.

Think about the apostle Paul, who wrote the vast majority of the New Testament. Prior to his life with Jesus, Paul was dedicated to killing Christians, and ending Christianity and its foundation. Then his road-to-Damascus experience changed his heart. He realized he had been fighting for the wrong thing, and this guy Jesus really was who he said he was. The same passion and the same determination that he used to kill Christians transformed him into helping the Christian church flourish across the world.

Paul wrote, "I don't really understand myself, for I want to do what is right, but I don't do it. Instead, I do what I hate. What a wretched man I am."

For a guy whom God chose to write the majority of the New Testament, to make such an honest confession is astounding. How many of us can say it? Think about your own personal struggles. We all have those times when we struggle for answers and hope. We all know there are some things we shouldn't be doing, but we do them anyway.

All those years ago, the apostle Paul wrote about the same struggles we all go through today, because they're timeless and part of human nature. Knowing that the people in the Bible were real and flawed like us inspires me, because they changed the world. None of us is perfect or knows God's plan for us, but it's important to remember that He never used perfect people for anything important.

SQUEEZE EVERY MINUTE
OUT OF EVERY DAY

It's hard for me to say no. It's not so much that I can't say no, but that I don't want to say no. Life is shorter than we realize, and I've already spent enough years wasting time and opportunity.

There are two reasons that motivate me to make the most of every day. The first reason is that I regret not doing things differently when I was younger. I wasted a lot of time when I was younger. Now, looking back at that, I think, "What if?" But you can't live there. I don't want to say, "What if?" anymore about anything. I just want to move forward.

The second reason is seeing all the unfulfilled needs in the world. They're almost endless. For many years, I've been involved with veterans' causes as well as supporting first responders, police officers, and firefighters. Now my focus is also on kids, the homeless, and underprivileged families. People gave my family opportunities and a leg up. We were never on government assistance, but that doesn't mean we didn't get help.

People helped us out of the goodness of their hearts, and there are so many needs out there that I could help fill. Often, I feel as if I'm wasting time if I'm not doing something. An offshoot of that is that I want to be as big an influence on the lives of my grandchildren as my grandfather was on my life. A lot of my time—which never seems like enough—is invested in them.

I don't need or want to save the world. I just want to have an impact. The biggest impact I'm going to have is on my family. It's probably the same for you. I want to be a good influence on them. I want to be a good role model. I want to be a good memory, like my grandfather is for me. I want to have a legacy that will live on twenty years from now. It's something we should all want.

Now that I'm older, I'm not looking for that making-the-whistle feeling that came from riding bulls, when I felt ten feet tall and on top of the world. Now, that feeling comes from being a good friend, brother, father, and grandfather. It comes from trying to do my job the best that I can. It's one thing to show up and just do your job. Given everything there is to talk about in the news, to go on the air and fill four hours isn't that difficult. Excelling at the day is always the goal.

Make no mistake, I'm not always successful. I'll go two or three days and realize I've just been getting through the days instead of taking control of the days. That's disappointing. Going back to my friendship with Glenn Beck, he's a great example of someone who makes the most of every day. In 2013, he came to Phoenix to give a speech on a Friday night. I was working afternoons, so I sent him an e-mail that said, "You're coming Friday. I'd love to get together. I'll take the day off if you've got time to get together for lunch."

He sent me an e-mail back saying he would be on the ground for only about three hours. He said he was giving the speech and then flying overnight to DC. He had three events in DC on Saturday.

I replied, "All right, I get it. Hopefully next time. It would be great to see you whenever you get a chance."

Ten minutes later he sent me an e-mail saying, "You know what? I have room on the plane. Why don't you fly with me Friday night to DC, spend the day with me on Saturday, and then fly home commercial on Sunday?"

Now I'm a guy who has never flown first class. I've flown coach every time I have ever been on an airplane. Now I was going to get on a private jet with Glenn Beck and fly to Washington, DC. I was blown away. I wrote back, "All right, I'm in."

So I went to the venue here in Phoenix, he gave his speech, we jumped in the car, we got on the plane, and we flew overnight to DC. We landed in DC early in the morning and got to the hotel at about seven thirty. Nobody slept. The first event was at nine thirty later that morning. We got to the Capitol, and there had to be at least a thousand people who showed up. He gave this huge, amazing speech. Afterward, he talked to attendees and took pictures with everyone who asked. He signed every autograph. He engaged with every person who wanted to talk to him. This was all during the fake government shutdown and there were no workers, so along with all of us, he grabbed trash bags and we collected trash to clean up the National Mall.

None of us slept while we were on the plane, so we were running on fumes at this point. After leaving the National Mall, we walked to the World War II Memorial to greet the Honor Flight groups. It's a great program that brings World War II veterans to DC to see the sights, including the memorial dedicated to them. As Tom Hanks said when it was being built, it is "a national memorial to honor the sacrifice of ordinary people who, half a century ago, did nothing less than save the world."

Glenn spent over an hour talking to World War II veterans. These guys were touching his face and telling him, "We love you for what you do." Glenn had tears in his eyes because these were veterans from "The Greatest Generation."

From the World War II Memorial, we went to an event in DC where he was the keynote speaker. We hadn't slept in 36 hours, and I was dying. Meanwhile, Glenn had a stack of books you couldn't see over with little name cards in each one of them, so he could autograph and personalize them. He signed every book. Then, he took pictures with all of the people backstage. Pat Gray, a host on TheBlaze network, and I left the backstage area, went into the audience, and sat off to the side. Glenn came out onstage and it was like a tent revival. He had people jumping out of their seats and screaming. Pat and I were sitting there falling asleep in our seats because we were wiped. The applause was waking us up. I complain about my schedule. I complain about my responsibilities. But that trip was the craziest thing I've ever seen. As I said, we joke that when you travel with Glenn, nobody ever sleeps. At the same time, he's somebody who understands the idea of squeezing every minute out of every day.

I've got a career that many people would envy, but I look at Glenn and think I could be doing much more with the time I have. That is always the carrot out in front of me. It's not the fame or the money. He is so selfless when it comes to interacting with people. It's a genuine part of who he is. I want to be like that. I want interacting to be about everybody else and their experience.

He's the one who lives it. I'm just the guy who looks at him and thinks, "I'll never complain about my schedule again."

I don't want to miss a minute of life. If I sleep six hours, that's a great night's sleep. I usually sleep four or five hours a night. I'm terrified of missing out on something or wasting the time I have left. I look back on my life, and if there was one thing I could ever change, it would be to make the most of my time when I was younger.

Remember when you were a kid? The school year lasted so long. Summer was never going to get here. Or it was never going to be Christmas. It just felt like it was going to take forever. Then we got to be the age when we're still writing last year's date on our checks.

I realize now at that I'm probably two-thirds through my life. So, I've got a third of my life left and it's racing downhill. The most precious thing you have is time. Invest your time in the people and activities that are most important to you.

DON'T LISTEN TO PEOPLE WHO GIVE YOU EXCUSES NOT TO SUCCEED— THEY HAVE THEIR OWN AGENDA

AS YOU KNOW BY NOW, if there's one local activity I love doing more than anything else, it's talking to high school kids. I love that age group; it's one of the reasons why I coached high school football. They're the coolest age of people to interact with because they are still idealistic. They're not total cynics. They haven't had to fight the world yet, but they are beginning to think like adults. I love that time in their lives.

I get to speak at Red Mountain High School in Mesa, Arizona, a couple of times a year. As I mentioned before, I don't find it valuable or interesting to give a standard speech. I let the kids ask questions, and I answer as best I can. At one event, a girl asked about wage inequality and the idea of a woman struggling in a man's world. I said to her, "You are always going to have people in your life who say you can't, whether it's because of the color of your skin, your gender, where you come from, or some other reason. If you listen to them, you are never going to accomplish anything. In America, we celebrate people who have been told they can't but do something anyway. If there's something in your life you want to do, you have to do it despite what other people say to you."

There has to be that inner voice inside of us all that tells us what's right and what's wrong. When a goal or career decision seems right to you, you must be willing to stand up and say, "This is right." If it goes against the people who are closest to you and alienates friends, you must be able to say, "I am satisfied that I know I'm doing the right thing."

That's why I said to this student, "You can do anything you want. I've got two daughters. I want them to feel like they can do anything they want. So don't let somebody else's judgment, opinion, or lack of motivation dictate what you can and can't accomplish. You can accomplish anything you want."

Unfortunately, nearly every conversation on equality is really about politics. If you disagree with Barack Obama, you're told you're racist. If you voted against Hillary Clinton, you're told you're sexist. They make those accusations to excuse a candidate's flaws, whether they are personal flaws or philosophical flaws. Hillary Clinton has been an accomplished woman her whole adult life. She had no business complaining about the glass ceiling after Donald Trump won the election. Her given reasons for losing did not address her campaign flaws. They did not address her past.

People who point the blame at others and make excuses for their failures want to keep others from succeeding so they can continue to make excuses.

ALWAYS SPEAK FROM THE HEART

I HATE WRITTEN SPEECHES.

Usually at a wedding, the best man and maid or matron of honor have to give a speech. It's usually the maid or matron of honor with a written speech, because women put a lot of thought into it. The guys, including the best man, just do it off-the-cuff because they're still hungover from the night before. How many times have we been to a wedding where the maid or matron of honor was standing there with a microphone in her hand and a glass of champagne in the other hand? She was probably also fumbling with notes for her speech. This is crazy to me. The bride was probably her sister or best friend. When this happens, I think, "Just tell her what you think." Rather than looking at the bride or the couple, she was looking down at a crumpled piece of paper. It makes me crazy. Whatever is said in the moment will be ten times better than anything a person could write down ahead of time.

You should try to connect with people when you speak, whether it's a toast, a job interview, or in an auditorium. Last year I was the keynote speaker at an event in Arizona with Senator Jeff Flake and Congressman Paul Gosar. Yes, I was just as surprised as anyone else.

I could have been intimidated and written a speech, but I'd rather speak from the heart. I've had the chance to see a lot of top-level speakers, guys like Rush Limbaugh, Glenn Beck, and Donald Trump (before he became president), go just from notes or nothing at all.

When you speak, there should be a core message you want to convey. You might need bullet points to stay on track, but don't rely on anything that's too confining. Of course, there are instances, such as when a president speaks on behalf of the nation or on a big policy pitch, when it's appropriate to have a written speech. One of the reasons Donald Trump as a candidate got huge audiences in person and on TV is because his speeches were unpredictable and not canned. It was smart not to do the typical speech of political platitudes, because everyone knows that's not him.

When you're speaking, don't try to be someone you're not. If you have a sense of humor, don't stifle it. Talk about your personal experience if you think the audience can relate to it.

I've been one of the people sitting in the crowd. I've always been that person up until a few years ago. I was a talk radio listener. I was somebody who would go to an event and listen to Sean Hannity speak. That experience made me a better speaker. I've sat in those chairs. Before speaking, I think, "What does somebody sitting in that chair need to hear? What's the most authentic way I can give it to them?" It's as simple as that. I don't have any expectation of success. Every time I get up to speak, I think they're either going to yawn or they're going to laugh.

I want to communicate with people the same way I would if I were sitting around with friends. There shouldn't be any pressure in expressing yourself.

For me, the common theme when I talk is independence, because I believe it's something we've lost—individually and as a country. The Founding Fathers realized that "absolute power corrupts absoloutely." The Founding Fathers were extremely independent. George Washington and Thomas Jefferson were completely different people, but they came together for a common goal. At the Constitutional Convention, the delegates couldn't get a Constitution written. They were all independent-minded people who thought there were so many things that were important that they couldn't agree on all of them. So, somebody rode to see George Washington and said, "We need you."

Washington said, "Listen, I've done enough. Haven't I done enough?"

But after contemplating the situation, Washington said, "You know what? I have done enough, but the work's not done."

So he rode to the Constitutional Convention, and they wrote a framework for the greatest country in the world.

These were independent people. Many of them could have lived out their days in wealth under British rule, but instead they risked everything for independence for future generations. That spirit should be celebrated, not scorned.

If you and I were in that position to cast votes in Congress, I might say to you, "I have an idea. I think we need to do this. This is the problem. This is the solution. Here's the legislation. Can I count on your support?"

Then you would read through it and say, "You know what? That's a great idea. I'm in."

Now let's say six months later I come to you and I say, "I have this issue I need you to support." This time you say, "I can't support that."

I'm going to walk away wishing I had your support, but I'll still have respect for your opinion. There's independence in all of us. We have to know what's right and wrong in our hearts and be willing to stand up for it, as well as accept it in other people. We have to understand that other people may not feel the same way, and compromise when we can. There's no reason to hate each other because you won't do what I want you to do. In politics, we have too much of a tribal mentality right now. We don't think independently. It's all about acceptance in a group.

It's easy to talk about this issue, because it's one I feel strongly about. You should feel the same way about whatever you're talking about, whether it's at your best friend's wedding or about a job you're passionate about doing.

"BLUE COLLAR" DOESN'T MEAN UNEDUCATED

ONE OF MY FAVORITE PEOPLE to watch and follow is television and podcast host Mike Rowe. In 2017, he posted on his Facebook page a letter he received from a guy named Chuck who tried to equate speaking up for blue-collar workers with the white supremacy movement. Chuck wrote:

> One of the tenants [sic] of white nationalism is that college educated [sic] people are academic elitests [sic]. Comment? No? I'm not surprised. You never take a political stand because you don't want to alienate anybody. Its [sic] bad for business. I get it. But there is a current of anti intellectualism [sic] in this country—promoted by Republicans.

It is one of the most ignorant things I've ever read. Content aside, you'd think that a guy claiming to speak against anti-intellectualism might run a spell and grammar check on a letter before he sends it.

Mike Rowe gave a fantastic response. Here's an excerpt:

mikeroweWORKS is a PR campaign for the skilled trades. For the last nine years, we've partnered with numerous trade schools, raised millions of dollars for work-ethic scholarships, and called attention to millions of jobs that don't require a four-year degree. But that doesn't mean we're "anti-intellectual." We're not even "anti-college." We simply reject the popular notion that a four-year degree is the best path for the most people. And we're hardly alone.

Millions of reasonable people—Republicans and Democrats alike—are worried that our universities are doing a poor job of preparing students for the real world. They're worried about activist professors, safe spaces, the rising cost of tuition, a growing contempt for history, and a simmering disregard of the First Amendment. These people are concerned that our universities—once beacons of free speech—now pander to a relatively small percentage of students who can't tolerate any political opinion that challenges their own. And they're concerned—deeply concerned—that millions of good jobs are currently vacant that don't require a four-year degree, or any of the catastrophic debt that comes with it.

On the issue of equating the white supremacy movement with his foundation, and on Chuck's logical fallacies, Rowe wrote, "A flaw in reasoning or a mistaken belief undermines the logic of a conclusion, often leading to real-world consequences. And right now, logical fallacies are not limited to the warped beliefs of morons with tiki torches, and other morons calling for 'more dead cops.' Logical fallacies are everywhere."

"Blue collar" doesn't mean uneducated. To think that is pretty uneducated. I'd like to see how far Chuck could get in his day without a blue-collar worker's applied expertise. If he wakes up to an alarm clock that runs or charges on electricity, he should already be thanking someone who chose a trade rather than a four-year degree.

I worked on construction sites with people who were brilliant and of all colors. Just because they wear jeans and T-shirts to work doesn't mean they're any less intellectual than someone who wears a suit and carries a briefcase. It is ignorant for someone who claims to be educated or an elitist to make that assumption. Chuck is the perfect example of someone who puts politics above leadership. In a failed attempt to feel superior, he's actually showing his ignorance and shortsightedness.

There are lots of men and women who could have flourished in academia. Instead, they chose to pursue a trade or some form of education other than a four-year degree. I guarantee you Chuck couldn't grab a toolbox and follow me or anyone else around a jobsite for a week.

Using a toolbox instead of a computer doesn't mean blue-collar workers have a lack of intellect. It just means they are people who have a different skill set. Many of them are very skilled in their area of expertise. Many of them are very specialized. As I said, I've worked with people who are brilliant at what they do.

If you take a guy out of academia and put him on a jobsite or in any of the millions of jobs available in the trades, he's going to be in over his head. If you take a guy off a jobsite and put him in an upper-level college class, he might be similarly lost. They are two different worlds, but one is not a more viable, relevant, or necessary path to success than the other. A blue-collar worker generally has more respect for academia than academia has for blue-collar work. Chuck is proof of that.

There isn't enough credit given to someone who just works every day. That's why I think Mike Rowe is one of the greatest voices out there today. Through his TV shows, podcast, and Facebook series, *Returning the Favor*, he's promoting a solid work ethic, opportunities for success, and the people who help the community without asking for anything in return. If there is one person whom I want to emulate, it would be Mike Rowe. He is one of the smartest guys out there. He is one of the kindest and most respectful people around. He's not a poser. He speaks for Americans in a way that is eloquent and shows the world that just because you put a toolbelt on every day and go to work, doesn't mean that you can use only small words and can't be a success.

Some of the smartest people I've ever known are people who do "dirty" jobs for a living, and some of the best advice I've ever gotten has been from them. My grandfather was my hero, and he was an auto mechanic. I learned my trade from people who have made a very, very nice living and became fairly wealthy by American standards. They have a mind for business and customer service. They are the salt of the earth, and they treat their employees like family.

I blossomed when I became an electrical apprentice and learned that trade. I saw a way to make a living by challenging myself and using my hands. I wasn't learning in a classroom, but every formula in the electrical contracting world is an algebraic formula. There are a lot of measurements, and you need to use addition, subtraction, and algebraic formulas for wire size and conduit size. You have to be able to do math equations using a pencil and a piece of paper to get the job done. Yeah, you're wearing a toolbelt, work gloves, and work boots, and you're sweating. If you're like me, you feel good at the end of the day because you're able to see what you've accomplished.

I grew up in a family of working-class Democrats. My uncles were Teamsters. One uncle worked as a baker for a grocery store chain, and the other one was on the loading docks of a major trucking company. They worked long hours. They worked hard. I think that even they would scoff at the liberal elitists who believe they are the ones who are intellectually superior. I would rather be around someone who values hard work than someone who values intellectual elitism and politics.

People like Mike Rowe and the men and women he highlights in his shows, *Somebody's Gotta Do It* and *Returning the Favor*, embody the leadership we need more of in our communities. There is no political posturing, just good, honest people who see a need in their community and decide to do something about it.

RESPECT FIREARMS—
AND TED NUGENT

WHEN I WAS IN MIDDLE SCHOOL and high school, Ted Nugent was a god. I had a friend who would carry the album *Cat Scratch Fever* to school every day. That's how much my friends and I loved Ted Nugent. *Free-for-All* was always my favorite Ted Nugent song and album.

Almost every summer, Ted Nugent performs at the Celebrity Theater in Phoenix. It's a big deal for his fans. Ted said how much it means to him that Arizona has been so open to him. He feels like it's his second home. According to Ted, "I'm really connected to those working-hard-and-playing-hard people of Arizona."

Even though another station was promoting the show, I wanted the political Ted on my show while he was in town. I wanted the Uncle Ted you hear on TV and on his social media. I was in the middle of a segment when he got here. It was surreal when all of a sudden Ted Nugent walked into the studio and sat

Ted Nugent in the KFYI studio.

down. He gave me a look like, "Oh, don't worry about it, just keep going. I'll talk to you in a minute."

Like it was no big deal. I thought, "That's Ted f—ing Nugent!"

When we talked during the break, I asked which topics we could talk about on the show. He said, "Listen. Let me tell you something. We can talk about anything you want. Nothing's off-limits."

He was so laid-back and relaxed. We turned that microphone on and he was Ted Nugent. There was no change in personality. He's the real Uncle Ted. He's going to tell you exactly what he thinks. There are no canned answers. He just grabbed the microphone and sat back for over an hour. We talked about everything. It was so much fun because I remember thinking, "That's not

Ted Nugent the rock star. That's not Ted Nugent the hunter. That's just Ted Nugent." It felt like I was sitting around with a bunch of my buddies at the house. It was like going on the air and saying, "Hang on a minute, I want you to meet somebody," then I bring Ted Nugent into my living room. As Ted said, "We have so much fun, it ain't right."

Obviously, one of the most interesting and entertaining issues to talk to Ted about is the Second Amendment. He's on the National Rifle Association's board of directors and is an avid hunter and conservationist. He's not shy about going head-to-head with people who disagree with him. As he said on my show, "Truth and logic can't be beat. Whether it's Piers Morgan, Anderson Cooper, or Bill Maher, or anyone else who tries to take me on, they always have, and they always will lose. They can't win against truth, and I have unlimited evidence, unlimited historical evidence on my side."

It's very important to me that my loved ones respect and know how to use firearms. Whether they carry is up to them, but they need to have the knowledge and skills they need to shoot. There are a lot of great places to go shooting in Arizona. Exercising our Second Amendment rights is so much a part of who we are that the issue isn't that divisive like it might be in other parts of the country. One of the things we do as a family is go out to the desert north of Phoenix. We'll set up targets and spend the day shooting. We buy practice ammo, bring food, and practice firing handguns and rifles. I want my kids and grandkids to be proficient in handling firearms.

It's interesting to see the differences between men and women when shooting. Men are tighter and tense. Women are more supple and relaxed. When you pull the trigger, it has to be almost a relaxed motion. Men anticipate the trigger pull and the boom, and we end up jerking the trigger back. One of the ways to practice with a pistol is to have a dummy round. You put the dummy round mixed in with all the bullets you're going to put into the magazines, so you don't know where that dummy round is going to be. If you feel yourself jerk the gun back while firing but it doesn't fire, then you realize you're anticipating the kick instead of just pulling the trigger. Men really are notorious for that. We'll squeeze really tightly in anticipation, while women are a little bit by nature more relaxed. I heard a rumor that Ted's wife, Shemane, is a better shot, but I'll never say that to his face. I suspect he's the kind of guy who would take pride in that, though.

The misconception about firearms is that it's an issue that's important only to men. That is just ridiculous. Not only do women tend to be better shots, but firearms are also extremely important for safety. You can't go a few months without hearing a great story about a seventy-year-old granny fighting off a bad guy with a shotgun. God bless her.

COMMON SENSE
TRANSCENDS TIME

A 1933 ARTICLE IN *Harper's* titled "What a Young Man Should Know" was particularly interesting to me because, despite being written nearly a century ago, a lot of the advice is still relevant. The article is pretty "hoity-toity" and there are some comical lines, such as "To my eye, an American who cannot throw and catch a ball seems pathetic and grotesque."

According to the author, these are the things every young man should know:

Leaving all formal subjects out of consideration, he should learn how to:

- Swim
- Handle firearms
- Speak in public
- Cook
- Typewrite
- Ride a horse

- Drive a car
- Dance
- Drink
- And speak at least one foreign language well

Take swimming. You start with the survival skills. You start with being able to go to the bottom and bounce your way back up to the top and float. Then you learn to swim in the shallow end, then in the deep end. Eventually you learn to dive and give assistance to someone else. Being from Florida, I've always been a good swimmer.

What's interesting about the 1933 list is that it's a little bit of the old and the new. In 1933, not everyone had a car, but men back then should have still known how to drive a car. Not everyone had a typewriter, but they should have still known how to type.

Today, we're almost going in the other direction, because there are kids who can text really quickly but are not as good at typing. It's the same with driving a car. There are kids in cities who use public transportation, friends, or Uber to get around. They might know how to get behind the wheel of a car and know the basics to get a license, but haven't driven since they got their license. They might not even know how to parallel park, since many states no longer make it part of the driving test. As the saying goes, "common sense isn't so common anymore."

It's never a good thing to have a sheltered existence. We may be specialized in what we do in our lives and careers, but we should be well-rounded and have the life and survival skills most of us don't need until we need them. It's good to have the urban and rural skills. Using a firearm, riding a horse, and swimming would fall into the rural category. In the time when the article was written, using a typewriter, being able to cook, and being able to speak in public might have fallen in the urban or sophisticated category. There's a huge world out there, and you don't want to miss any of it.

I saw a good example of when a rural skill might be of use during the coverage of Hurricane Harvey in Texas. Several rescue organizations put out a call for people who could help get horses to safe ground. This might include knowing how to put a halter on a horse, being able to put a lead rope on it, ride a horse, and lead a horse to safety.

It always feels good to use these skills to help other people, but self-sufficiency is also important. If I must write a business letter or résumé, I want to be able to do it without asking for help. My grandfather was such a great auto mechanic, but automotive technology has gotten to be so advanced now that it's all computerized. However, it's still useful to be able to diagnose a problem by process of elimination and, as I wrote earlier, know the basics like how to change a tire. Knowing a little bit also helps you pick the right person for the job.

Just like packing a bug-out bag that includes items for rural and urban environments, you should have a diverse set of skills that can be used when you most need them.

HOW TO MAKE A GREAT STEAK

I'M A VERY BASIC COOK. I can cook all the basic meats—steaks, hamburgers, and chicken. Any of those things I can cook pretty easily, but it's basic family comfort food. I'm not a gourmet by any stretch, but I know enough to cook healthfully for myself. Knowing how to cook a quick, healthy meal is helpful because it keeps you out of the drive-through lane.

I worked in restaurants starting at the age of twelve. I was cooking in restaurants beginning at the age of fifteen. I am very good at all the things that people don't think about when they're cooking dinner at home. One of those things is timing.

It's ironic, because timing is what tripped me up on my first radio show when I didn't know anything about hard breaks and posts. I already understood it from working in kitchens but wasn't used to applying it in radio.

While I'm cooking dinner, I want the side dishes and potatoes done when the meat is done. I want to make sure that if I'm sautéing mushrooms and onions, the onions are caramelized and the mushrooms have soaked up the butter. I want everything to be hot and ready to be served at the same time when the steaks come off the grill.

The easiest way to control timing when cooking is to have all your ingredients prepped. That's really important for me, because I like my steak very rare. I don't want to be slicing onions and mushrooms when the steaks have only a few minutes left. Prep everything and have your grill or pans hot and ready. Have whatever spices and aromatics (garlic, ginger, shallots, and so on) you use cut and ready to go. You don't want to be three-quarters of the way through cooking a meal, and realize you don't have pepper or that all you have is a moldy garlic bulb.

If you're cooking your meat on a grill or in a cast-iron skillet, turn it just once. Don't press it hard enough for any juices to run out. Touch your meat as little as possible. (This is also good advice for politicians and Hollywood producers.)

After you take your steak off the heat, let it rest for a few minutes. Don't immediately cut into it, because you'll lose all those good juices. I'm a purist when it comes to steak, but don't worry about breaking rules. Eat it however you like.

Finally, clean as you go along so you don't have a pile of dirty dishes and utensils sitting in the sink longer than they should.

My life is so hectic that I have to maintain some semblance of order at home. When you don't have that accountability of living with other people, you might find yourself with a mess piling up. You don't want to come home one day and think, "This is like an episode of *Hoarders* around here."

There's something to be said for discipline. I'm always on time for work. I rarely take a day off unless I'm really, really sick. If I say I'm going to be at an event, I'm there even if something else comes up that I'd rather do. I go to the gym. I eat fairly clean.

But then when I get home, stuff piles up. It's partly because my home is basically a crash pad. I'm rarely there except to sleep. It's important to make sure you keep things in order, because it's a reflection of you and how you're going to start and end your day.

WATCH ONE, DO ONE, TEACH ONE

THERE'S AN OLD MEDICAL SCHOOL adage that goes, "Watch one, do one, teach one."

You watch somebody do something, then you do it yourself, and when you're proficient enough at doing it yourself, you teach it to somebody else.

As an electrical apprentice, I had the opportunity to watch, then do. When I became a foreman on a jobsite, the manager of a department, and then the owner of my own company, I got to teach someone a job skill. I went from doing something myself to teaching somebody a different or faster way of doing something so it saves him or her some time and trouble. It's very gratifying to pass knowledge on to someone else. I went from being a high school dropout to being a good enough electrician that I was able to teach people something that would make them better at what they did.

Now I hear from people who are much more interested in how to get into broadcasting. I talk to high school students about it, and every once in a while, I'll get an e-mail asking for

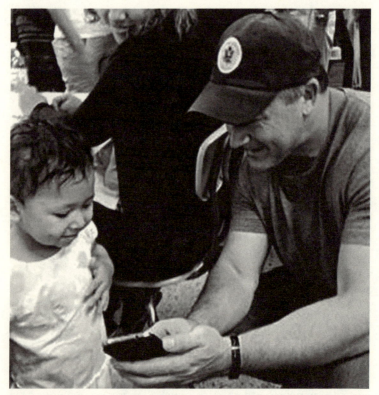

Doing relief work with refugees in Texas. I enjoyed showing this little girl photos of my grandson.

advice. The only sincere advice I can give is what I did—you should do what you love enough to do for free. If you love to speak in public or if your dream is to be on the radio, do it for free. Somebody will let you do it for free. As you develop the skill and you're good enough, you'll get paid to do it. If you're really good, you'll make a career out of it. If that doesn't happen, you're still lucky enough to be able to do something you love in your spare time.

Every coffee shop and bar singer out there with a guitar is singing wherever and whenever he or she can. If those singers love it, they work their butts off all week long making money to live. Then, when they get the opportunity on Thursday, Friday, or Saturday nights, they go to the coffee shop or bar down the street to sing their heart out. That's happiness—doing what you love. If you're good, someone will want to pay you to do it because that person realizes he or she can make money from what you're doing.

Every one of my bosses saw my skill set as an electrician. I did my job because it was self-fulfilling. I worked hard all day, accomplished the job I was given, and paid attention to detail because it made me feel good. My job was to make them money, but I did it for me. The same goes for my career in broadcasting. I didn't get into it because I could make some money. Somebody gave me the opportunity to do a radio show. I did it for free for eight months before anybody paid me a penny to do it. Then I made next to nothing from 2005 to 2009. It wasn't enough to live on, and no disrespect to those who paid me, but it was akin to a street musician leaving his guitar case open for donations. I was basically getting a gratuity.

I went from doing my first radio show for free in 2004 to getting paid a small amount from 2005 through 2009 before I got a radio contract. Even after getting a contract, I still had my electrical contracting company because it wasn't enough to pay bills. It wasn't until 2010 that I began to shut my business down and was able to make a living in radio. That's almost six years. In terms of timing in the broadcasting field, that's relatively short. But that's an example of putting in the work and it eventually becoming the thing that pays the bills.

Another example is bull riding. I loved the cowboy lifestyle. There was something about bull riding that was not just physically challenging but also mentally challenging. I just thought it would be the coolest thing in the world. I visited Arizona in 1992 on vacation for the first time and saw bull riding in a bar. There was a live bull in the bar. I thought if I ever had a chance to live in Arizona, I would give it a try. In 1994, I got the opportunity. Thanks to the skills I had as an electrician, I was able to pursue something I loved without having to rely on it financially. So in February of 1995, I moved to Arizona and pursued the dream of being a rodeo cowboy. As I said earlier, I worked as an electrician and a company manager on weekdays, and I did bull riding on the weeknights and weekends. I never did it professionally or for a living—I wasn't good enough. I've already told the whole story earlier in the book, but I got to have this incredible experience because I met some people at a bar and said, "I just want to learn."

I've always been so open to learning because a lot of times those experiences first come from a parent. All of those little things that are between a father and a son, I never really did. I think if my grandfather would have been alive as I went through school, things might have been different. It didn't mean much to me then, but now when I look at my kids and grandkids, I think about the things I missed. Maybe I would've been a much better student and graduated from high school at the top of my class if I'd known my grandfather was going be there to watch me walk the stage. He would have been the guy I would've wanted to go to a bar with who would buy me my first beer. I know those are small things, but those landmarks in your life that are very personal are usually special because of who you're sharing them with, not because of what you're doing.

One of the biggest compliments I've gotten in my extended family has been that I remind them of my grandfather. There is no bigger compliment to me. I never really thought about it until I sat down to write this book, but my grandfather and I have one really important commonality. We both lost our brothers in a war. My grandfather had a brother who was drafted into World War II. His brother didn't want to go, and my grandfather said, "You're going. No one in our family dodges the draft. You go."

His brother was killed in combat. My grandfather lived for the rest of his life with the fact that he convinced his brother to go to war. I never knew that story until I got older and I found his brother's medals in the closet in their bedroom. My grandfather had his brother's, my uncle's, Purple Heart. Every time I open the box with my brother Tom's medals, I think about being a young boy and finding that Purple Heart my grandfather kept. I think about the legend that my uncle must have been. If my grandfather were alive to see what my life has turned into because of what happened to my brother, I think he would be proud of me because he understands the pain from that kind of loss. I think he would be proud that from that pain, I've found a purpose.

One of the greatest benefits of teaching is not just passing on knowledge, but also showing someone that he or she is valuable. My grandfather made me feel like I was important even though I was just a goofball kid. Everybody needs to have one of those people in his or her life at some time, ideally at a very formative time, to give him or her a base of self-esteem. Teaching can be a good business investment, but more important, it's showing people they have value.

YOU'RE GONNA MAKE A MISTAKE WITH MONEY

MANY YEARS AGO, I was working with a guy a few years younger than me who was my apprentice on the job. We were in his personal vehicle driving to a jobsite. He wasn't paying attention to the road in front of him. He was looking at something else and didn't see that all the traffic in front of us had come to a stop. We hit the back end of a van going fifty miles per hour. We were going so fast that the motor broke off its motor mounts and came through the front of the truck.

I broke my shoulder on the dashboard and tore my rotator cuff. The side of my head instead of my face hit the windshield and left a big gash in my head. My apprentice's insurance company gave me a twenty-five thousand dollar settlement.

The advice I got from everyone was to put it away, pretend like I didn't have it, and forget it's even there. They said, "You're going to be amazed at how much money that is twenty years from now."

You know what I did? I blew it. I spent every penny of that money. I bought a new truck and put a three thousand dollar stereo in it. Instead of saving that money and putting it somewhere where I could never touch it, I basically spent it all in a few months. Now all these years later, it would be worth probably about two hundred thousand dollars if I had invested or done something else worthwhile with it. In the grand scheme of my life, it isn't the end of the world to have lost twenty-five thousand dollars, but I can't help thinking what it would be worth now if I had taken everyone's advice.

Looking back now as a fifty-one year-old man, I cringe thinking about what that money could have amounted to at the time if I didn't spend it. Unfortunately, I was too self-centered and looking too much for that immediate gratification to heed any advice from anybody around me.

It would be great if I could say that's the last mistake with money I made, but it wasn't. When I started making more money, I didn't pay attention to my federal tax withholding. I ended up getting myself into tax debt because I didn't do something as simple as change my withholding when I got a big raise and a big contract. Now, it's not millions of dollars, like Hannity or any of those guys have, but for me it was more money than I had made before. It was enough to put me into a different tax bracket. I didn't talk to a tax professional about it; I just kept going about my business. The next thing you know, I owed a big debt to the IRS, which I had to pay off over time.

In both instances, I made the same stupid mistake: not taking money seriously. When you have money, whether it's a little or a lot, you need to be responsible. You don't want to end up costing yourself down the road. That hurts way more than saying no to a short-term desire. It's also good to reach out to people who may have been through something similar. Unlike me at eighteen, you should probably listen to their good advice.

Don't beat yourself up too much over money mistakes because everyone makes them. In 2014, Arizona Cardinals cornerback Patrick Peterson received a signing bonus of 15.3 million dollars as part of his 70 million dollar, five-year contract. It became a national story when a reporter asked him if he had cashed the check yet. He said he hadn't, and when asked why, he said, "I just haven't gotten around to it."

Everybody became armchair accountants and investors. A math teacher estimated that in the twenty-seven days he took to cash the check, he could have earned over twelve thousand dollars in interest. If he had invested in a CD with a more aggressive rate of six percent, he could have earned over sixty-eight thousand dollars.

When you're an NFL athlete, you realize that your career is short-lived because you age much faster playing professional sports. Players want to squeeze every minute out of every practice and game. They leave the money aspect to other people or it's a secondary concern. Players live the lives of professional athletes. They buy nice cars and nice houses. The smart ones understand the money is going to end at some point and want to stay within their means so they can live comfortably after they retire. Others live like it will last forever and regret it later.

Financially, I've fallen into the "living the life" category more often than I should have. If I have a hundred bucks on Friday, the following Thursday I'll have a dollar in my wallet. Put a thousand bucks in my wallet on Friday, and I'll have a dollar in my wallet the next Thursday. After I lost everything several years ago, putting money away and making a commitment to building my 401(k) became a priority.

For someone in his fifties, I still have a long way to go before I can feel financially secure about my retirement. Fortunately for me, I'm making enough money that I can try to make up for some of that. For about a year, I didn't look at my 401(k). Then I checked it and saw the progress I had made over the previous year.

Ultimately, the best money advice I could give is to never let your immediate gratification get in the way of your long-term goals. It's funny because financially, I haven't always followed that advice often enough, but I have in other aspects of my life. I am pretty disciplined when it comes to going to the gym and watching what I eat. I can do those things because I have goals in mind, and indulging an immediate gratification is an impediment to reaching those goals.

BE FRIENDS FIRST

I ALWAYS SAY THAT I've been happily married a couple of times. I might not be an expert on relationships, but at least I've done the research.

The one piece of advice that I've found the most valuable is to be friends first. A genuine affection for somebody in friendship will last longer and also lends itself to respect. When negative emotions come up during a relationship, like being very selfish to protect your emotions, the friendship will win out. There are people in relationships who treat their friends better than they treat their partners. If that person is always a friend, then there's a genuine love, and so the other issues can be worked out. There may be a person that you really like, but is it based on a friendship? Is it based on what you know about him or her, or is it based on what you see? The great part is when what you see matches what you know about the person, and then you've got something really cool.

From a faith-based perspective, a great guy named Tommy Nelson teaches a series on relationships using the Song of Solomon. He basically says that you should run at your speed for God, then look around and see who's keeping up. The same can be said for anything else in life. Run at your speed and then look and see who's keeping up. Those are the people you want around you. They will be friends and allies during your successes and failures.

Friendship and admiration have to be there before the rest of it can work. There are lots of misconceptions about what men and women want. I can't speak from the perspective of women, but I can speak from my own experience. When it comes to dating, the whole midlife-crisis stereotype of dating someone twenty or thirty years younger doesn't interest me. There's no attraction for me there. I am attracted to somebody my age. I want people who have had the hell beaten out of them their whole life, and who come out of it with character. They are still attractive, and they wear their battle scars well.

I am attracted to women who get who they are and where they've come from. There is a definite camaraderie when you're sharing a life with someone like that. Attractiveness comes from confidence, accomplishment, and the worldliness you get from experiences. We all have baggage we drag with us, and it's cool to be with someone who understands you.

It's great when women come out on the other side and whether they've got children or grandchildren, and a career or no career, they still have confidence about where they are in life. I'm very thankful that I'm not the guy in his fifties chasing twenty-five-year-old women. I'm sure that there are twenty-five-year-old women who are very genuinely attracted to guys in their fifties. I'm single now, and I love being around women my own age. There are the music and movie connections, and shared pop culture references. There are the shared life experiences, like children, grandchildren, career choices, and other things that have happened over the years.

THERE'S SATISFACTION IN CREATION

THERE IS JUST SOMETHING ABOUT manual labor that makes you feel good. It's about creation and accomplishment. Whether it's cutting firewood, building something, or cooking, there is a sense of gratification that I get from looking at a finished product knowing that I did it. For younger generations, creation might be more tech-oriented. There may be kids now who are developing apps, but in the end there is still a sense of satisfaction that comes from saying, "I did that." Not "I paid for that." Not "I hired somebody to do that."

A while back, I put recessed lighting in my house. It might not seem like a big deal because I'm an electrician and that's what I've done my entire life. But trust me, when I get home after a long day, the last thing I want to do is climb on a ladder and put in lights. It's the work I had been doing all day. But I did it. It was done and it looked cool. It was nice to look around and have my family recognize, "Man, you're good at that." It was that satisfaction of saying, "You know what, I'm sweating for other people all the time. This time I sweated for me."

My grandmother was the sweetest little old Polish lady you've ever seen. As I said earlier, she cooked Polish food that was so good that I get hungry just thinking about it. She cooked her little butt off all the time. She got so much joy out of it. Her kitchen table was always covered in flour. She was always making dough for pierogi or my favorite, paçzki, which are like deep-fried doughnuts. I can't describe them any other way. The dough is thick and sweet, with raisins, and it's deep-fried in oil. Then you cover the paçzki in powdered sugar. They're so delicious. When she took them out of the oil, they were so hot that you couldn't pick them up, never mind put them in your mouth. Yet I would try to eat them immediately despite burning my mouth because they were that delicious.

My grandmother's pierogi were stuffed with mashed potatoes, sauerkraut, and some other stuff. She would make the dough herself and cook it in melted butter. There was always a huge serving bowl of freshly-made pierogi and butter. We would eat, and you could see how proud she was when our faces were stuffed. We thought we couldn't eat another bite, but we wouldn't stop eating. She got tremendous satisfaction in creating something for us. She used simple ingredients like flour and water and eggs, but everything she made was amazing. She knew that by the time we were done eating, we were ready to carry her out of the house on our shoulders.

My grandmother was a housewife. She never worked outside of the house. My grandfather was the patriarch of our family. For the brothers, uncles, and cousins, he was the guy everybody went to for advice. Everyone in our family surrounded my grandfather. But my grandfather would tell you that my grandmother was the backbone of our family. She cooked, she cleaned, and she took care of everyone. She was just this loving, kind, hard-working person who cooked like a dream.

We all have different talents. We get the most satisfaction when we use those talents to create things for ourselves and for others, whether it's an app, a pile of cut firewood, or paçzki and pierogi.

DON'T LIE IN A JOB INTERVIEW

DON'T LIE. DON'T DO IT to the person who is interviewing you, and don't lie to yourself. When in a job interview, we tend to want to give the answer we think the interviewer wants to hear. Don't inflate your experience or lie about the things you know how to do.

If the interviewer asks you a question about how you would handle a situation, answer honestly what you would do. If the person disagrees with your answer, you don't want to work for him or her anyway. You should be interviewing the interviewer as much as he or she is interviewing you. It's not arrogant to ask questions. It lets interviewers know you value the job, and your skills and career goals. Interviewing them about the job isn't just about what it pays and how many vacation days you get. You want to know about their management philosophy. Some people might like a lot of direction. Others prefer to be creative and left alone to solve problems on their own.

Good employers or bosses are going to ask you about your work ethic, your past experience, and how you work with other people. They want to know if you're going to fit in with the company. If you're serious about taking the job, then you want to know the same things about them. You'll want to know about the work-life balance, particularly if you have family obligations. Is weekend work expected? Is travel expected?

Ultimately, the decision is not just whether a company wants to hire you, but also if it's a job you want.

LEAVE A JOB BETTER THAN YOU FOUND IT

WE DON'T ALWAYS GET to leave a job on our own terms. If you are leaving a job or are given some time before a layoff, always try to leave it better than you found it.

Before I moved to Arizona, I worked for a company in Florida and got along very well with my boss. I admired him, and he was an amazing contractor. I learned a lot from the way he ran his business, his attention to detail, and his discipline with money. On the weekends we would hang out and play golf. We were friends, and he was good at differentiating between work time and weekend time. While at that company, I went from being a service guy to a field supervisor to a manager. I loved the job and working for his company, but an opportunity to move to Arizona came up and I couldn't pass on it.

When my annual review came up at the end of year, I said, "I'm moving to Arizona."

He said, "So you're not just using this as a tactic to get more money?"

"Nope, I'm going to Arizona," I said. "But I'm not on a timetable, so if you need me to stick around for a month, I'll stick around for a month."

It was early December, so he said, "Can you stay until the end of the year?"

"Absolutely."

I stayed, and around the end of December he said, "We're still really busy. How much more time can you give me?"

I said, "You want another month?"

I stayed on for the entire month of January, and he was grateful.

On Thursday, the day before my last day, he said, "Come in tomorrow, bring all of your stuff for work, and bring your golf clubs."

On Friday, we checked out my vehicle, I gave him back all the company tools used on the job, and we went to the nicest golf course in town. We played a round of golf and he took me to lunch. The last thing he said to me was, "If you ever want a job again, you've always got a job with me."

It was one of the best compliments I've ever received. All I did was say, "You've been good to me, and it's no skin off my nose to stick around. I don't have to leave on any timetable."

That's really the best way to leave a job. You won't always have the same circumstances, especially with time, but giving two weeks or more of notice and making recommendations, or helping with the interview process for a replacement, will go a long way in people's minds, especially if the person you replaced didn't do any of those things.

For me, being fired is a lot like being broken up with in a relationship. There are many times when the relationship isn't good for whatever reason, and it just depends on which person does the breaking up. You either get fired or you quit. It just depends on who ends it first, so if it wasn't you, you must let go of that feeling that you didn't do it first. In the end, it wasn't a good fit, and with that realization you can move forward.

START A BUSINESS BECAUSE YOU LOVE IT, NOT BECAUSE YOU NEED TO MAKE MONEY

EVERYONE HAS AN IDEA of what it would be like to run his or her own business. If you want to be a business owner because you want to make a ton of money and have a bunch of free time, you're fooling yourself. It's going to take a lot more time than you ever imagined, and it's going to be less about running a business and more about babysitting.

I loved being an electrician. I loved the idea of everything involved with a job, from giving clients a price on a job to giving them a final bill, and leaving them happy with a project. However, it is all of the things you wouldn't imagine that come along in between that drive you crazy.

Maybe you have this idea in your head of what kind of an employee you are. You expect everybody else to be the same responsible employee. Instead, as a business owner and boss, you find yourself spending an inordinate amount of time dealing with employee squabbles as opposed to making the business decisions you think you should be making. Managing human resources is just adult babysitting. Don't interrupt people. Don't touch what isn't yours. Be fair. Clean up after yourself.

When owning a business, particularly in its infancy, you realize you're going to risk everything on every job. In the business I was in, the profit margin on jobs is not extremely high, you've got a ton of money at risk, and you have to hope your employees do the right thing. You have to rely on the inspectors doing the right thing in the inspection. You have to hope your customers pay bills on time. There are so many things riding on the success of just one job that are outside your control. You have to be really good at the things you can control, because those other outside things can come along through no fault of your own and screw up every bit of your success.

Among the things outside your control are the whims of local, state, and federal governments. Regulation compliance is so expensive and stifling. If I wanted to start my contracting company back up again, first I would need to rent an office building. I'd likely have to renovate it. I'd have to buy a bunch of trucks. I'd have to hire people. I'd be investing tons of money into the community and economy. Then the government would come along and say, "Well, here's your list of compliance issues, and you're going to need somebody in human resources in your office for compliance."

That would cost me forty thousand dollars a year. Then the local government would change the regulations on something like the placement of electrical sockets or training methods.

Work would stop, or there would be the cost of changes to existing projects.

By this far in the book, you know me and won't be surprised that I made some mistakes with my business. I was a good electrician. I had good connections in the industry. I had a good reputation. So, I made the decision to go out on my own. My company was able to get work, and it grew pretty fast. At one point, I had eighteen electricians working for me, and the business was going along okay. I didn't have any money, so all the money to run the company had to be borrowed. I took a mortgage out on my house. It was the time when banks just were throwing money at people. I got a fifty-thousand-dollar line of credit on my house, among other things, to expand my business. Instead of growing slowly and saying no to some jobs, I said yes to everything and tried to make it work.

When the economy took a turn in 2008, construction basically dried up in Arizona. I went from having a bunch of people working for me to having nobody working for me. I was underwater and didn't have enough money in the bank to pay employees and pay our monthly bills. Getting out from under that debt was daunting. Fortunately for me, my radio career was taking off at the time the market was crashing. I was about two hundred and fifty thousand dollars in debt. I was up all night and wasn't eating. I lost eighteen pounds in fifteen days.

I went to my creditors and figured out a way to pay my debt down over time. It took me a couple of years. Last year, I finally paid off one of the last of those lines of credit. It's one thing to pay off a credit card, because your credit is still there. If you pay one thousand dollars on a credit card, you still have that one thousand dollars in an emergency. That's not the way it is with the debt I had from the business. When you owe fourteen thousand dollars to Home Depot, it's not like that money is available in the future. Everything got paid off. I didn't care about being broke. What I cared about was not being able to meet my obligations. That scared me. I didn't feel bad about short-selling my house, because we did everything we could to work with the mortgage holders and they didn't want to work with us. They basically told us to just walk away from the house, so I did. That was tough.

Coming from where I came from, two hundred and fifty thousand dollars seemed like an insurmountable amount of money. Just an unimaginable amount of money. It felt like I was never going to climb out from under it, and somehow I did.

The bottom line is that you should start a business because you love what you're doing, not because you need to make money. Grow slowly and pay attention to politics and regulation burdens because those could end up having a bigger impact on how well your business does than anything else. We should be allowing the small-business owners, who are the lifeblood of this country, do what they do best—innovate, employ people, and move America forward. If we would start deregulating and cutting taxes at all levels of government to a smaller degree, there would be more incentives for businesses to reinvest and grow rather than be at the mercy of politicians.

FIND YOUR PEACE

I ALWAYS SAY I don't need much sleep, but the funny thing is that when I do sleep, I definitely feel refreshed. The older I get, the less I think about external fulfillment. I don't need money. I don't need things. The one thing I do want in my life is peace.

When you're younger, you want excitement. When you're in your twenties and someone asks you, "What did you do this weekend?" you might answer, "Nothing" like it's a bad thing. Now that I'm in my fifties, if someone says to me, "What did you do this weekend?" I say, "Nothing" like it was an accomplishment.

To me, peace is not having any frustrations. I have responsibilities at my job that feel immense to me, because the people I work for have made it a point to show me that they want me to be the face of the radio station. Some people might see that as an accomplishment or a compliment. It is both of those things, but to me it's also a responsibility that I take very seriously. There are salespeople who make a living selling advertising time on the radio station. I know that there are people who count on that.

There are also the responsibilities we all have. My family counts on me, and I don't want to let them down. I hope I never do.

My family is in a good place. I'm in a good place. Work is in a good place. Feeling this way has been rare in my life. Often, I feel like my life is all about herding cats. I feel like Rocky chasing a chicken. You have to try, but you never quite get there.

There is some kind of an obligation, big or small, in every part of life that always seems to need your attention. Those moments with my grandkids are when everything feels like it's in order.

You're never going to be able to explain the feeling of finding quiet moments of peace to people who are young until they go through it. The best you can do is prepare them for it so they can appreciate that time when it comes.

BUYING BIGGER PANTS ISN'T THE SOLUTION

WHEN I WAS YOUNG, I could never gain weight. I actually wanted to gain weight. I wanted to be a bigger guy. I wrestled at 128 pounds during my junior year in high school. I was 140 pounds when I got out of high school. I couldn't play football as I got older because I was just too small. I was always that kid who bounced around at a weight that was easy and stayed in decent shape without having to try. I was also no stranger to the gym lifestyle, because I really enjoyed it. I loved challenging my body in any way. I worked with a trainer who showed me how to eat right, sleep right, and lift right. I slowly put on some pounds and developed some musculature as I got a little older. But weight and watching what I ate were never a problem—until they were.

When I hit my mid-thirties, two things happened. First, my metabolism really started to change, which is pretty normal as you get older. The other thing that happened was that my work changed. I was a guy who worked every single day on jobsites and walked a couple of miles a day. During the day, I was lifting materials and tools. I was working with my hands and burning calories like crazy. But then as a manager, I spent more of my day bidding and billing jobs, and doing paperwork. I put on about thirty-five pounds very, very quickly and didn't even realize it. I would just get bigger pants and not think about it. I had gone from wearing twenty-nine or thirty-inch waist jeans to being in relaxed-fit thirty-sixes and still needing a little more. I was looking at myself in the mirror when I got out of the shower and thinking I'd become Fred Flintstone. I couldn't stand what I saw in the mirror anymore.

I couldn't seem to lose the weight on my own, and I didn't know the reason why. I look back now and I think how silly I was. I would lie in bed at night and watch TV. I would watch *Jeopardy*, then I would watch *Judge Judy*. I would watch these TV shows while eating one of those big half-pound Hershey bars. Every night I would eat one of those. Then after I would eat a big candy bar, I wanted something salty. So, I'd eat half a bag of potato chips.

I'd get in that sweet-and-salty cycle. Then I would wonder why I couldn't see over my belly to watch TV and why the weight wasn't coming off. Coincidentally, one of my first endorsement clients for the radio show was a company called Medifast. The owners of the local Phoenix-area franchise, Marvin and Ilyne Fleischman, have become great friends since they came on board with the show. When I met with them, they didn't put any pressure on me to do the program, but I said to them, "I have to do something."

I ate the five Medifast meals every day for eleven weeks, and I lost almost thirty-five pounds with the program. I remember looking at myself while standing on the scale and weighing in less than 200 pounds for the first time in a long time. It was such an awesome feeling, and I didn't want to give up.

Obviously, my fear was that as soon as I stopped with the program and the premade meals, I would put all the weight back on. Thankfully, that hasn't happened. What it has done is motivate me in the other direction. I went from being 185 pounds or so and back to fitting in the thirty-inch-waist jeans to actually gaining weight because I was gaining muscle. Now I weigh almost 200 pounds, and I'm bigger and stronger than I've been in decades. I realize that my physical health is more important to me now because it's harder to achieve. Every slide back is harder to recover from once you get older. Now, I have to actually earn my health as opposed to just having a metabolism that races, the way it did in my younger years. But the other part of it is, at fifty-one years old, how long can I keep getting stronger? How long am I going to be able to bench-press 365 pounds? How long am I going to be able to keep up the musculature I have now? Every day that motivates me, and it matters to me that I still work on myself.

I actually feel better about the shape I'm in at fifty-one versus when I was twenty-five, because now I have to really put some work into earning it. At twenty-five, I didn't have to earn it. If I wanted to lose some weight, I'd eat only half of a Double Whopper instead of the entire thing.

I've always been a healthy eater for the most part. I love good, wholesome food. I love vegetables. There are not very many vegetables I don't like to eat. I love protein. I am a meat eater. I love steak, fish, and chicken. So, I eat healthy meals. My downfall was desserts. I was also a late-night eater. I guess there's something about the darkness and the glow of the TV that makes your mind think those calories don't count. Late at night I'd reach for the chocolate and the ice cream. Combining that with not burning calories on the jobsite, and I was packing on extra pounds before I knew it. Now I still have that sedentary work, maybe more so than before, and I realize I have to put in the work to keep the weight off. I don't deprive myself of the things I love; I just have to be smart about the choices I make.

Whether it's your career goals or personal finances, the principle is the same—don't let your short-term desire sabotage your long-term goal. When working in construction, fast food is your friend. You're driving from jobsite to jobsite, so you drive through Burger King or Wendy's because it's convenient. It's easier to eat a burger while driving from place to place than to eat a salad. So, you grab something to eat and you don't worry about it because you're working your butt off on a jobsite. You're sweating like crazy. Or maybe you're still younger and still have that killer metabolism. You're going to burn those calories off pretty quickly, so it's not that big of a deal.

Then your situation changes. You get older or you spend more time sitting than standing and walking around, but you're still making the same food choices. It's going to catch up with you. Financially, it's like when you're making a lot more money than you need for your bills. You have more disposable income and spend indiscriminately. Maybe you'll use valet parking more often or go out to eat more often. It's not a big deal because the money is there and those little decisions aren't important. Then your financial situation changes and you have to be more careful about what you buy and how you spend your money. In both situations, you wake up one day and say, "How did I put on all this weight?" or, "How did I get so far into debt?"

You realize you have to reel those desires back in.

There will always be temptation, whether it's to eat dessert, stay out late drinking, call in sick to work, or buy a new car when a used car is a better financial decision. There is never a shortage of want in the world, and you never grow out of it. When it comes to food, moderation can mean you taste everything but then stop after a bite or two. Now out of necessity and motivation, my long-term goals matter more than the short-term gratification of how good that dessert tastes.

After losing the weight and getting my eating habits under control, I started to get back into working out. I met Johnjay Van Es, from the national radio show *Johnjay and Rich*, which is based in Phoenix. Johnjay was training at a place in Scottsdale, Arizona, called Urban Garage Gym. He told me about his trainer, Mitch Lewallen, and said, "Man, this guy's awesome."

So, I met with the trainer. This guy is almost 10 years older than me, and he's built like a twenty-five-year-old. I explained to him that I've got injuries. Both my shoulders have been broken. I've broken my leg and my ankle a couple of times. I have sciatica. I told him I have all these medical issues, but that I really want to start training again. Mitch was amazing and said, "Let's do it."

He has shown me how to work around injuries. He has worked with me on building muscle mass, even at my age, and it's been the best experience. Again, it took dedication. It's never going to be easy. I had to be smarter about how to treat my body. Every day I go to the gym and I'm much more deliberate about everything I do, which makes me feel like every gain I make is well-earned.

I get a lot more satisfaction out of setting goals for myself. I used to hate working my chest, because I wasn't able to do as much as I wanted. So, when I pushed up to bench-press 375 pounds, that was a big day for me. That was almost an impossible goal. Like I've done in other areas of my life, I sought out and listened to good advice from good people, and was disciplined in what they said I should do. It was eat, sleep, lift. Now I train the smart way out of necessity and just love reaching for those goals.

YOU DON'T WANT TO LOOK GOOD FOR YOUR AGE

VANITY PLAYS A BIGGER PART in a man's life than most of us will admit. What's funny is that with women, it's acceptable. Women wear makeup. Women dye their hair. Women primp before they go out. It's accepted and, for better or worse, sometimes expected.

Guys always act like, "Yeah, whatever. I'll do the best I can." But we want to look good, too.

On "Throwback Thursday," I sometimes post pictures on Instagram of myself when I was younger to prove that at one time I had really good hair. I joke around and say, "My forehead has become a five-head."

I look at myself and I think, "What happened?"

Truth be told, I'm getting more comfortable with admitting I'm fifty-one, not twenty-five. I don't need to look like a twenty-five-year-old. I want to be the best-looking fifty-one-year-old I can be. I'd be lying if I said vanity doesn't play a part in it. I like the fact that I buy extra-large T-shirts because they're tight in the arms.

One of my colleagues at the radio station used to make fun of me because of my T-shirts. We were at a big meeting with our radio station, so there were probably seventy-five or eighty people there, and he cracked a joke about me wearing tight T-shirts. So, I cracked a joke too, saying, "You know what? You're right. My T-shirts are tight on the top. Yours are tight in the middle." He quit messing with me, but it was all in good fun.

To me there is no worse compliment than telling people they look good for their age. I don't want to look good for my age. I just want to look good. But I realize that time always wins. But that doesn't mean I'm not obligated to do the best I can at fifty-one. My trainer, Mitch Lewallen, is a good example of someone who motivates me to always try to do better. He pisses me off sometimes. He is a few years older than I am but in amazing shape. He has trained his whole life. He has never left the lifestyle. He has earned every gain. It's like people who have made a middle-class income their entire life. By the time they're fifty-nine, they have amassed a ton of money in the bank and are ready to retire. You think, "How the hell did they do that?"

Those people were disciplined their whole life and are now reaping the benefits at fifty-nine, thanks to all the work they did when they were twenty-nine and for the next thirty years. Mitch is the guy I go to for every bit of advice I need for training. He's the guy I lean on and admire when it comes to training. He has dedicated his life to doing the right thing when it comes to physical well-being for himself and for others.

I like to think that my vanity is a little deeper than just appearances. As an adult, I have always been that guy who challenged himself. So, if my boss gave me a stack of work orders and said, "I want you to get these done this week," I'd tell myself, "All right, I've got five days. I'm going to get it done in four."

Or on a building project, a boss might say, "We've got four weeks built into this project. Can you get this project done in four?" I would say, "I'll get it done in three."

When I got into radio, I promised my bosses that even though I wasn't the most talented person they'd ever met, no one would work harder than I would. That's always been my mindset, and so I want to go in to any situation being the best I can in that moment. When it comes to looking good and being healthy, there are some mitigating factors. We all have them. For me, I can't run anymore. My leg has been screwed together a couple of times, so the impact caused by running doesn't work for me. Both of my shoulders have been broken, and I'm limited in the athletic things I can do there. The one thing I can do is lift weights.

Being able to push myself and be better today than I was yesterday is important to me. The reality is that physically I'm not twenty-five anymore, and I'm really okay with that. I don't want to be twenty-five, physically. But the victory for me is that I feel like I'm the best fifty-one-year-old I can be. I'm as big and strong as I'm going to get, and I'm proud of that. I work hard. I get disappointed in myself when I let myself slack. If I tweak my shoulder or something happens that means I can't put 100 percent effort into a workout, I'm really disappointed. I don't feel like I have to be the biggest, strongest guy in the gym (I never will be, especially at Urban Garage Gym). I genuinely feel like I have to be as good as I can possibly be. There's only one person who can truly keep me accountable, and that's me. I'm

Fighting fifty.

the only one who can walk out of a workout knowing whether I had a great one and did the best I could, or if I slacked off and didn't do the best I could.

I genuinely don't do anything for anybody else. I want to be able to look at myself in the mirror and say, "I'm happy with what I see." It's mentally healthy to have the mindset of knowing I'm never going to be twenty-five again, and I don't want to chase a feeling contrary to that, because it would drive me crazy. It would be impossible to not realize that, because regardless of what the mind thinks, the body has the tendency to remind us of the truth.

Unfortunately for me, because I'm an insomniac, I rely a lot on energy drinks, and it really did some pretty significant damage to my body. I ended up in the hospital on New Year's Eve with chest pains thinking something was wrong with my heart. It turned out that my blood pressure went through the roof and my kidneys weren't working. When the doctors and the nurses did some investigating on my habits and found out that I was abusing energy drinks, they decided those were the culprits. I was trying to maintain a level of energy I wanted to have, but I was doing it unnaturally. When I weaned myself off the energy drinks, my blood pressure went back down to normal. There's no easy path. I know my lack of discipline regarding my sleeping habits rears its head and smacks me back to reality. The reality was, I was cheating my body on the sleep it needed and trying to overcompensate by using energy drinks.

Vanity isn't about looking like someone else's ideal. There was a sort of culture moment when the media declared that women prefer a "dad bod." In a 2017 Planet Fitness poll, seven out of ten women thought a softer, less muscular "dad bod" was sexy. Forty-seven percent said it's the "new six-pack."

People have to be happy with what they see in the mirror. I've always been an athlete, and I'm happier now than when I had my "dad bod." I still have my limitations. The impact of jumping out of the bed of my truck onto the ground causes excruciating pain. I can run only about twenty-five yards before the pain bothers me. I never play the "Turkey Bowl" on Thanksgiving. The only thing I can do to challenge myself now is go to the gym and lift weights, and that gives me a lot of personal gratification.

In the previous chapter, I mentioned that I bench-pressed 375 pounds. What I didn't mention was that my goal for my fiftieth birthday was to bench-press 400 pounds. I bench-pressed 375, and then I injured my shoulder. I never hit the 400-pound mark. But at fifty years old, I bench-pressed 375 pounds.

Satisfaction and sadness come with being in your fifties and lifting weights. The sadness is that you don't recover as quickly. You get injured more easily. Gains, including muscle gain, are a lot harder to come by. But the satisfaction is that in spite of those three things, I'm still bigger, I'm still stronger, and I still feel good when I'm able to keep up with some of the younger guys in the gym.

There's a saying that the best time to plant a tree is twenty years ago. The second best time is now. Whether you're trying to lose weight, trying to gain muscle, trying to save money, trying to buy a house, or trying to get out of debt, you have to just get on it. If six months from now you're better than where you were, that's awesome. You can't compare yourself to where others are in those areas. You just have to focus on your progress and on being in a better place than you were.

Setting goals is an important part of feeling that accomplishment, regardless of your age. To just wallow and get through the day without thinking about tomorrow or planning for tomorrow leads to a stagnant life. I don't ever want to be stagnant, and you shouldn't either.

FOR THE POLITICIANS:
NOT EVERYTHING IS YOUR BUSINESS

WHEN I WAS GROWING UP, my mom's side of the family was pretty tight-knit. The uncles and aunts would get together once a week and play cards or play pinochle. Some of the guys would have a beer or two, but then they would have coffee and dessert and play cards until ten or eleven o'clock at night. I always hated going to bed, because I wanted to sit around with the grown-ups while they were talking. I don't remember any political conversations. I was politically motivated as a kid, so I would have actually remembered them.

When Jimmy Carter ran for president in 1976, I wrote him a letter saying I liked him and was trying to get my parents to vote for him. I have no idea what it was about Jimmy Carter that appealed to me as a little kid. My politics are pretty clear now, but I think Jimmy Carter is a good man. He's a good man and the worst president of my lifetime, possibly with the exception of Barack Obama. After Carter won, I actually got invited to the inauguration. I got a letter in the mail when he won, and we went to his inauguration. As it turned out, my parents didn't vote, but we went to the inauguration anyway. The next inauguration I went to was forty years later, when Donald Trump was sworn in as president.

Republican, Democrat, or Independent, I have the same message for all politicians on all levels of government: not everything is your business. Every piece of legislation that is proposed should start with the question, "Is this any of the government's business?" That would stop 90 percent of the useless, time-consuming junk they vote on. A lot of the legislation that makes somebody feel good, or satisfies somebody's urge or need to "do something," does nothing but create another pile of paperwork. At some point, someone should stand up and say, "This is none of our business." That would be so refreshing.

Former Congressman Ron Paul was known as "Dr. No" because he tried to follow that principle. He was the lone "no" on a lot of votes. He said he voted only for things that the Constitution authorizes Congress to do. The media would focus on his voting no against a Medal of Honor for Rosa Parks, while ignoring the fact that he also voted no on medals for Ronald and Nancy Reagan. Where he fell short is in the explanation to the general public of what that meant and the bigger picture. Ron Paul went a lot further in politics than I ever would, but you have to tell people what voting no means to them and why that philosophy on voting and the Constitution matters to the average American. His supporters seemed to know, but outside of that dedicated support, others didn't know his philosophy. They just knew him as the guy who voted against Rosa Parks and against breast cancer research. The principle was lost.

The First Amendment is another issue that needs a more nuanced explanation. In our current political and media climate, if people say that the neo-Nazis and the white supremacists have the First Amendment right to march in Charlottesville, they're lumped in with the neo-Nazis. When I was younger, the photographer Robert Mapplethorpe was a big deal. His photographs were very controversial, and were all protected by the First Amendment. There was also an art piece by Andres Serrano shown on a tour that was partially federally funded through the National Endowment for the Arts, and it was called "Piss Christ." It was a photo of a crucifix in a jar of urine. It was meant to stir emotion. Well, if that's protected speech, then I'll defend it. I don't want to pay for it, though. I've also defended people who burn the flag. I think burning the flag is the most reprehensible, offensive thing you can do to so many people on so many levels. But it's Americans' protected right to do it. As stupid and as arrogant as it is, they have the First Amendment right to burn the flag. Millions of Americans also have the right to criticize those actions.

Somehow, "shock art" got to be totally predictable. It's all about dumping on the American flag. There's an art gallery that has the American flag hanging out of a toilet. Another art gallery uses the American flag as a doormat outside its door so you have no choice but to step on the flag on the way inside. All of that is protected by the First Amendment. As ridiculous, uncreative, offensive, abrasive, and inflammatory as I think it is, it's all protected. But so is the speech by the people who offend flag desecrators (and most Americans)—white supremacists and neo-Nazis. No one has a right to be violent, but people have a right to express their views. That's what the First Amendment protects—what we all find offensive on one level or another.

I can see how it must be hard for politicians on either side not to get sucked in by the mob mentality and the call to "do something," especially when they see an issue that offends them and their supporters. Make speeches. Tweet your thoughts. But before you get the government involved, ask if it's any of the government's business.

FOCUS ON WHAT YOU CAN BE

IN A RARE INTERVIEW on Fox News, Supreme Court Justice Clarence Thomas said that he had a sign in his office with a saying by his grandfather. His grandfather raised him and had no time for excuses. The sign says, "Old Man Can't is dead and I helped bury him."

It's a great philosophy that I've unknowingly tried to follow my entire life. It was usually motivated by someone telling me I couldn't do something and wanting to prove that person wrong.

When it comes to my speaking and broadcasting career, I never had the expectation that I would be successful. There was no pressure on me to be a spectacular speaker when I spoke at my brother's memorial. All I wanted to do was communicate a message from our family. When it came to speaking on my brother's behalf on radio shows and at other events, I never expected anything to come of it either. All I knew was that my brother deserved to have his story told.

Once I got a regular radio gig, I always thought the bosses were going to hire a professional some day. I thought, "Someday, they're going to figure out what a dope I really am." I was always prepared for that. As my mom always said growing up, "If you're gonna be dumb, you better be tough."

This gave me the liberation to not care. I was able to do everything for fun because it might not last. I wish I could say there was a disciplined plan involved. There wasn't—if I had a plan, I'd sell it. Instead, I focused on what I could do, and that was to tell my brother's story. I didn't care if I got up onstage and made a fool of myself doing it. I thought that at some point, when they laughed me off the stage, it would be a funny story to tell.

At the hardest moment in my family's life, I had to focus on what I could do. At that moment as we pulled in front of the hospital for the press conference after Tom's death, the one thing I could do was speak. I have never, ever been afraid of public speaking. I don't know where it comes from. For a short time, I went to a Catholic school. I was in third grade, and we had the traditional Catholic mass. There were two readings, and then the priest did the Gospel and homily. I was chosen to do one of the readings. Everybody thought it was such a big deal. They thought I was going to be afraid. I remember thinking, "What's the big deal?" I thought, "I can sit down and read a book, so what's the difference if I'm standing and reading it out loud?"

I got up and did the reading. When it was over, the principal (who was also the school's priest) recognized me and said, "What a great job you did."

I thought it was the easiest thing I'd ever done. As I started doing more things as an adult, I was free to fail because whatever I was doing wasn't my job. I did it as a hobby. It wasn't tied to my making a living. It's like dancing. I don't care if I make a fool

Speaking at "People Over Politics" in Gilbert, Arizona.

of myself dancing, because I'm not losing any money. I don't work at the Fred Astaire Dance Studio. I don't have to be a good dancer. I dance because it's fun.

I'm no different than anybody else. If I can carve out this career for myself, then anybody can. We live in the greatest country in the world, which lets you achieve all of your aspirations if you're willing to do them for nothing. We get the pursuit of happiness, unfortunately not the pursuit of happiness and money for it.

We are all dealt a hand of cards at different times in our lives. We don't ask for it. Good or bad, something is handed to us.

You always have to do the best with what you've been dealt. Tom Brady is going to go down in history as the greatest quarterback who has ever lived. That began with being a fifth-round draft pick. When he got his opportunity to play, he did the best he could with it and it worked out.

I'm never going to be an NFL quarterback. I'm never going to be Rush Limbaugh. I'm never going to be Glenn Beck. I'm never going to be Sean Hannity. I'm never going to make tens of millions of dollars via a radio contract. But who cares what I'm not going to be? I want to find out what I *can* be. I just need to be the best I can be, and if I can do that, then I can go to bed at night. That's all that matters. You have to maximize your potential. You will be infinitely happier and more successful if you focus on your unique abilities and goals rather than trying to outdo someone else.

The good news is that every day we get the opportunity to discover a new talent. One of the things I've learned about myself is that I'm really good under pressure. I didn't know this until a crisis hit my family. I take a lot of pride in the fact that when there is a problem in my family, they come to me, particularly because my grandfather was that person in the family before he died. I don't take that responsibility lightly, and I'm honored by it. My brother, my nieces, my nephew, my sister-in-law, my mom, my kids, my grandsons—when times get tough, I'm the one they're going to call. Their faith in me means a lot.

IT'S NEVER TOO LATE TO CHANGE

ONE MATH PROBLEM I REMEMBER having to figure out in elementary school was how old I would be on January 1 of the year 2000. I figured out I was going to be thirty-two years old in the year 2000. I remember thinking that at thirty-two, I was going to be an old man. I couldn't fathom being thirty-two. Now I would kill to be thirty-two.

Now that I have a different perspective, I want to make the most of the years I have. At forty, I started lifting weights. I'm now the happiest I've ever been. I work out in the gym like a maniac. As I said, I'm in better shape at fifty-one than I was at twenty-five, and it means more to me now because it's harder but much more rewarding.

I have to be careful though, because I'm just as stubborn as I was when I was younger and riding bulls. Now I'm still stubborn, but older. Last year I hurt my shoulder at the gym. I needed to go to the doctor and knew I would possibly get a cortisone injection for the swelling. I told myself it would be okay and I didn't go. I also didn't want the doctor to tell me to stay off it for a couple of weeks. Eventually, my shoulder bothered me so much that my workouts were affected; I couldn't work out in the gym for seven weeks. I would do half a workout and leave, barely able to move my arm.

Finally, I went to the doctor. The doctor said, "We're going to do a cortisone injection." The staff did an ultrasound, put the needle in my arm, did the injection, and within three days my arm felt so good. I thought, "Why didn't I do this seven weeks ago?"

I immediately got back to working out and started to put a little bit more muscle back on again. I'm never going to be as muscular as I could be if I were twenty-five, but I can be a lot more muscular than I might otherwise be at age sixty. You shouldn't limit yourself based on what you think you can't do because of your age or circumstances. Instead find out what you can do in spite of those things.

At fifty-one, I find it's more of a necessity to treat my body better. I can't go to the gym and not warm up without the possibility of an injury. I can't just push weights around and gain a bunch of muscle. I can't eat like crap and not gain any fat. What I can do is go to the gym and be as big and as strong as I can be in my fifties. That shift in perspective helped me immensely, because now it's about what I can still accomplish.

When it comes to changing, there's a difference between flaws and limitations. I've got a three-inch vertical, meaning I can't jump any higher than three inches off the ground. I can't run because of injuries from bull riding. Becoming an NFL linebacker was physically impossible. That's a limitation.

A flaw is something like lying or procrastinating. Those are things you can try to change or at least work on to reach your goals. My limitation is time. My flaw might be that I

At the Wildlife World Zoo with my two oldest grandsons.

procrastinate. If there is something that I know has to be done (like make a book deadline), I may scramble for the last two days like a maniac because I've been procrastinating. To overcome my limitation and flaw, I have to think about the importance of my goal.

My mom is in her seventies, and I want this book in her hands. I want my other family members, especially those who never got to meet my grandfather, to read it. I want my grandkids and others to know about my brothers, Tom and Bryan, and understand that they are heroes, along with my mom. The documentation matters to me. I also want people to relate to the book. I would love to get an e-mail from some young person somewhere in the country saying, "I read your book and it stopped me from doing something that could have messed up my life." Or, "It motivated me to do something I always wanted to do."

I would love that, and it would mean more to me than being on some bestseller list. I coached many years ago and every once in a while, I'll hear from a kid I coached who now has kids of his own playing high school or Pop Warner football. He'll call me Coach, and it makes me feel so good. I can look back at that and know that I influenced somebody.

I wrote this book because it was the right thing to do for my family and for the legacy I want to leave behind. If people read it and love it, man, that's going to be the icing on the cake. If it doesn't sell even a hundred copies, I'm still going to be okay. The publishers won't be, but I will.

At the end of your life, you want to be comforted by the thought that you chose what to do with your life and that you didn't settle for anything less.

ACKNOWLEDGMENTS

TO MY GRANDFATHER FRANK KLIMA: Thank you for the example you set, the time you spent, and the wisdom and love you provided. The memories are some of my best, and they were the only things I had to hang on to in some of my most difficult days.

To my mother: Thank you for your work ethic and strength. For doing the impossible with three crazy boys. I know I wasn't easy, and I am sorry for so many things. But I am so happy that we are the family we are.

To my brother Bryan: You are truly my hero. There isn't a person I trust, love, or respect more than you. It has been the greatest honor of my life to call you my brother.

To my brother Tom: Your quiet strength and honor were seen by so many. You influenced so many. I wish I could have seen your face the night they renamed our high school stadium after you. I miss you more than you know. I can't wait to hug you again.

To Elaine, Blake, and Raven: You have forever changed my life. I wouldn't have survived some of my darkest days without you. You have been a part of some of my best days, too. With the addition of those four amazing boys, I can never thank you enough.

To Glenn Beck: It has been an honor to have you be like the big brother in my family. You have shown me how a big brother should behave. Thank you for your generosity, humility, example, and commitment. My career wouldn't be where it is without you. But more importantly, you've shown me how to be a better man. Thank you for that.

To Lisa De Pasquale: Thank you for tolerating me throughout this process. I would not have said yes to writing this book with anyone else. You are amazing.

ABOUT THE AUTHOR

MIKE BROOMHEAD is the #1 morning-drive radio host on KFYI and host of a weekly television news show in Phoenix. Prior to his broadcasting career, he was an electrician and winning bull rider. He is the father of two daughters and grandfather to four boys.